Desert Honey

Copyright © 2021 Desert Honey Project LLC
Photographs copyright © 2021 by Desert Honey Project LLC
All rights reserved.
Published and printed in the United States of America. No part of this book may be used or reproduced in an manner whatsoever without written permission except in the case of brief quotations embodied in articles and reviews.

For more information, please contact lizwescott@deserthoneyproject.com
ISBN: 979-8-9852487-0-8 HardcoverEdition

Desert Honey

Recipes of Comfort and Nostalgia by a Desert Rat

Written by: Elizabeth Wescott
Contributing Authors: Amy Ramsey and Sharon Bateman
Cover Art and Photography, and Publishing
by: Elizabeth Wescott

A CREATION OF DESERT HONEY PROJECT LLC
WWW.DESERTHONEYPROJECT.COM

Table of Contents

Appetizers 1-27

Fire Grilled Artichokes with Aioli, "Baby Crackers" and Caviar with French Shallot Mousse, Blue Corn Fried Okra, Bratwurst in Puff Pastry, Giant California Roll, Fried Panela with Herbs, Heirloom Tomato Salad, Laura's "Crispy", Pimento Cheese, Blistered Shishito Peppers, Spam Musubi, Steamed Pork Dumplings, Rainbow Carrot and Whipped Feta Tart with Orange Blossom Honey

Main Events and Some Things on the Side..........................32-84

Amy's Lazy Braciola, Parmesan Mashed Potatoes, Bean and Bacon Soup with Pimento Grilled Cheese, Braised Short Rib, Pasta Carbonara, Chicken Katsu, Lighter Eggplant Parmesan, Elote Cornbread and Abarriata Chili, Escargot, Filipino Hot Dogs with Chili Crisp, Chorizo Dogs with Black Bean Whip, Perfect Sushi Rice, Roast Chicken on Toast, Mom's Chicken Divan, Mom's Clam Linguini, Janie's Rice, Janie's Southern Squash Casserole, Shrimp and Grits, Fried Chicken with Chinese Hot Mustard Vinaigrette, Edemame Spaghetti with Cilantro Pesto, Honey Smoked Spareribs, Smoked Crab Legs, Onion Jam, Mac N' Cheese and Braised Short Rib Sandwich

Breads and Baking.......85-102

The Best and Most Versatile White Bread Recipe, Blueberry Cream Cheese Babka, Orange Blossom Cream Honey and Meyer Lemon Babka, Shokupan, Bao, Flour Tortillas, New York Bagels, Perfect Pizza Dough

Desserts..........................105-140

Arroz Con Leche, Baked Bosc Pear with Salted Honey Whip, Meyer Lemon Cookies, Pound Cake, Honey Toast, Leche Quemada Ice Cream with Vanilla Bean, Miss Moffet's Brownies, Lemon Turmeric Tart, Mochi Donuts, 'Melt In Your Mouth' Cookies, Sweet Mojito Mint Ice Cream, The Sub Shop Cookie, Butter Coconut Cream Cakes, Vanilla Bean Pan Dulce, Beauty Bowl, Yeast Donuts

Cold Drinks....................143-152

Coachella Valley Date Shake, Mosaic Coconut Milk (non-dairy), Red Clover Iced Tea Lemonade, Cashew Cream Cinnamon "Ngg", Mexican Frozen Hot Chocolate, Cold Brew with Salted Honey Whip

INTRODUCTION:

The Venn diagram of 'People That Write Cookbooks' and 'People Like Me' would only show me in the overlap. My sister is an award-winning pastry chef and a very talented cake decorator who has been creating stunning wedding cakes for over a decade. Her hard work and extremely long hours on her feet in the abusive workspace of a Las Vegas Bakery that has long since closed honed her unique talent of being able to ice a wedding cake in butter cream to such perfect smoothness in seconds flat (It's no wonder that fellow employees in our kitchen space would pause with heavy boxes in their arms to watch while she worked this impressive magic) Rugged bakery life also prepared her to own her own successful operation later on. She should be the one writing a cookbook but her much less technically skilled, non-culinary school-graduate younger sister has questionably assumed the role.

When I was in college at UNLV in 2011, my sister started her own wedding cake business and hired me as her baker. This was exciting to me although I was going in with no knowledge of wedding cakes, high-volume baking, or experience with being paid to make a food item. My prior work experience in the food industry started when I helped open a Latin restaurant on the Las Vegas strip. The training was quite interesting and immersive as we spent the better part of a week learning about the origins of types of Latin Cuisine, sugar cane production, and the agriculture of Argentinian wine. When it was time to open a mostly outdoor concept in the middle of a frigid January, things seemed to quickly fall apart with this new restaurant as they often do in the industry. All of this was unexpected and disappointing to me, but none so much as the frequent and aggressive sexual harassment by other staff that always left me stunned and unsure what to do or say since I didn't want to complain - ridiculous, I know, but I was young and intimidated. I was fired

anyway when they cut staff down try to stay open. This was a significant teaching moment in my life in the sense that there is nothing to gain (personally or professionally) by allowing yourself to be disrespected. The truth is that my experience is not unique and the restaurant industry treats women the absolute worst of any line of work I have ever been in, hands down. I left it in the dust, but not all women working in it want to or can. They certainly shouldn't have to especially for these reasons and those that want to contribute their time and talent to it should be able to do so in peace. Leaving a toxic environment is always the right choice, however, and ultimately, doors do tend to open. This was true for both my sister and I as we started a new business renting kitchen space from a wedding venue that we were contracted to as a vendor.

I often jokingly compare working in a bakery to working a construction job. Lifting thirty-pound buckets of ingredients, fifty-pound boxes of shortening, and forty-quart metal mixing bowls is no easy task. You are always dirty; covered in frosting and sweat. Your hands look like a box of markers exploded on you while you were holding them. These were hard days sometimes, but we worked exactly when we wanted, and laughed a whole lot. I gained about thirty pounds overnight and made a bunch of money. All we had to consider was the head cook, Maria's schedule as we shared her kitchen space. Maria ran a tight ship in her kitchen, and she bore the work of cooking an entire dinner service for wedding parties, usually more than one in a day and ranging anywhere from 50 to 275 guests. She worked smart and somehow managed to stop and make us lunch even on very busy prep days which usually consisted of her version of street tacos or soup. One day it was 120 degrees in Las Vegas in the afternoon and the air conditioner was struggling. Maria served us some of her extremely spicy and boiling-hot fideo soup. It's the closest I've ever been to actually being on fire, but I loved every second of it. My sister and I agreed that we'd rather die than ever refuse Maria's cooking only because we appreciated her kindness so much. Maria was a great influence on me for many reasons and she showed us some cooking methods that became standard practices in my life. She was very welcoming to us and commended us for being hard workers. She so sweetly agreed to provide the dinner for my own wedding and gave me the warmest hug on the day of. Those were truly the best days.

It's been ten years since Amy and I worked together and said goodbye to the bakery life. This experience shaped my love for cooking and baking, and I feel that through food and sharing knowledge, we can connect and learn from others. Food is the way I connect with other cultures; being invited to a dinner table always feels like a generous gift to me and I get immense joy from returning that kindness. Growing up, preparing meals as a service to those who were sick or in need was a common practice for my mom. She is known for her sweet deeds and beautiful food gifts. To me, this is an art that is getting lost in an increasingly busy world and yet becoming all the more valuable: the giving of thought and time to another. Her charitable spirit is an inspiration to me and my four older siblings.

As I get older, I have learned to cherish those very old pieces of paper that my great grandmother, Jaqueline-Inez (we call her 'Ganny') wrote her recipes on. Part of her legacy was her giving her heart and soul to cooking delicious southern classics and luckily for us, she took the time to write her recipes and hand them to her grandchildren. I feel connected to those that we've lost when I remember them by making the recipes that they loved and trusted. Few things in life provide such comfort. My mom is from North Carolina and my dad is from Virginia, and our strong southern roots provide some well-loved family recipes originating from the depression era which I will share in this book. My mom is a historian and authored the first published poem about the Vietnam War.

My dad is a piano business owner and a published author as well. Their wisdom for life and hilarious way of storytelling is unmatched to me. Meanwhile, I can hardly remember what I ate yesterday but they can recall specific details and events from their childhoods in the 60's.

VEGAS

In 1998, when I was 10 years old, we moved to Las Vegas from Michigan which was a bit of a culture shock. This place was incredibly hot, dry, and unlike anything we were used to, however, there was an incredible offering of Mexican food here and it was a delicious melting pot of some of the greatest cuisines and restaurants the world had to offer. There are not many cities in America where you can live in a mundane suburb and only drive about 7 miles before you hit at least a few Michelin-starred restaurants, among other things. It wasn't uncommon for my mom to take my sister and I out to a Mexican restaurant right after school or somewhat late at night on a weekday. My mom introduced me to and taught me to love Mexican food which, if lightly pressed, I would say I am most passionate about. My dad, having traveled extensively to Japan and Korea for business, introduced us to sushi and taught us polite dining practices. How to eat in such a way that shows respect to the chef serving us. I tried to flex this knowledge on my friends at school and socially, it wasn't my best work (the eye patch that I had to wear and being way too into The Mummy made me a tough- sell in a new school). When we weren't looking for crab legs on the weekends, we were at some Prime Rib special at a small run-down roadhouse casino or having all-you-can-eat spaghetti at a 50's diner where an Elvis impersonator would perform on Saturdays. We were also introduced to a 24-hour town and a culture that can't easily be defined because it's made up of so many different things. In all honesty, it took more than a decade for me to like living here but now as I've had my own child here, I consider it home. There is a hive of things to be discovered in this city and exploring it never really ends because of its rate of growth. Our China Town is a frequent dining and grocery shopping haunt of mine because it is a dense hub of some of the more unique dining experiences and home to the some of the best dishes I've ever tried. But the doorway I like to darken most is the Cuevas Meat Market because they have the best meat selection and sell some of the most gorgeous produce in the city. Not to mention a delicious secret Taqueria and panaderia hides in the back. It is a hidden gem. I could marry it. Going up Boulder Highway a little further, you will arrive in Boulder City, which is a charming little town that is frozen in time. It is home to the Hoover Dam and Lake Mead as well as many historically significant sites and markers. The town itself is picturesque and has a mid-century aesthetic. It's a lot like Palm Springs but with a more Southwestern feel. This place is home to many friends of mine and I spent several years familiarizing myself with its winding streets, small shops, and antique odds and ends. A more purist idea of Southwestern culture and history exists there and people who live in it can enjoy a small escape to the past.

We live in a truly odd and unique place and some of the lifestyle aspects have become indispensable to me. There is an underworld and a diverse mix of people here. People in this community are something to be experienced because most people came from somewhere else and have a story of what brought them here. Artists, restaurateurs, musicians, professionals of all kinds make up this strange and great city. Yes, it is the actual surface of the sun in July, but you are welcome here because everyone is weird here.

DESERT HONEY

Bees of the desert are a unique breed as they can withstand incredibly hot temperatures. The honey that these bees produce, known as desert honey, is a fascinating substance culminated from the diverse species of desert flowers that the bees pollinate. Desert honey is known for its uniquely powerful healing properties and is used often in medicine and even in wound healing. It also provides many kinds of amino acids and free radicals, making it known throughout time as a super healing food. In a raw and unfiltered state, it is dark and has a rich distinct flavor that can be added to almost anything you make as a secret ingredient for complexity. I use this ingredient in many of these recipes as it is a food staple in my life. I enjoy buying it whenever I see it being sold at farmer's markets or sourcing it from friends of my parents who are beekeepers in Phoenix. It is truly a liquid gold product of nature. Beekeepers in the southwest do important work to preserve the health of the vital species that produce it. It's a fascinating process and the poetry of it has inspired many analogies in literature.

This book is so named in the literal sense but also the figurative sense. This diverse community of strength and solidarity can be found in the most desolate places and that is a sweet reward. The Sierra Nevada Desert is one of the harshest landscapes in the country. The dry heat and record-breaking temperatures render this place borderline uninhabitable in my opinion and I curse it by making a solemn oath to move to a cooler climate every summer. But in the biome that resembles what I imagine Mars to look like, there is something unique to be found here. There is a diverse and rich community in this city made up of hard-working families and individuals, outside of the neon raucous gambling and entertainment epicenter that it's known for. This community alone was faced with the unfathomable tragedy of Route 91 in 2017. As a trauma nurse working nearby, I'll never forget the event and the aftermath, but what particularly stands out is the incredible amount of support and gratitude that we received from our community. The outpouring of support was overwhelming in the best possible sense and reminded us that what we do is important, and that while our work is demanding, it is also extremely vital to our community. Las Vegas showed a courageous example of healing after tragedy and those of us that experienced it either as a victim, a first responder, or as a citizen, are bonded in that experience forever.

ABOUT THIS BOOK

Baking is my background in professional food experience, but I am self-taught in cooking and every bit a humble home cook. I didn't even have a blog prior to writing this cookbook. Typically publishing a cookbook is the next step for a chef, celebrity, successful YouTuber or blogger with some level of fame and notoriety, The fact that I am hungry, I love to cook, and I think other people are hungry and love to cook too is what brought me in to this space. I buy and read cookbooks all the time and my collection would bury me if it fell on top of me. I am no one and this book isn't particularly specialized. Perhaps only specialized in the sense that most of what I have created here are dishes and recipes that pull me into some of my favorite memories growing up. For me, that refers to the restaurants and places I've ventured to from coast to coast, including the places in LA. that I visited with my best friend Desirée (who lives there and works on big animated movies- I live through her and it shows) The recipes are also reminiscent of my incredibly memorable travels to New Orleans and Punta Cana - The Dominican Republic with my bestie and partner in adventure, Allex. We traversed the tropical countryside to the chocolate plantations and experienced Arroz con Leche made by a local woman who lived on the plantation. It was transcendent. Recreating these experiences, or some from my favorite restaurants is something I love to do. These recipes are mostly forgiving and versatile, meaning if you want to change or add something there is flexibility. They are a tried-and-true assortment of my favorite things, and my favorite things are generally not ground-breaking but I hope that you can use this book to satisfy a craving or to learn the basics of some classics that may not be in your rotation. Not to replace but to add to your indices. Above all, have fun in the process of cooking at home and enjoy the fruits of your labor with others. Do this as often as possible and I promise that your life will be richer for it. We all have a creative spirit inside of us regardless of what it is we do daily for a living. Share your talents with others because the world needs them. I am excited and grateful that I live in a time where if you want to create something beautiful and share it with others, you can and there isn't a lot of red tape standing in your way. Those of us that are tired of simply consuming and are ready to create are freer than ever to do so and that to me is incredibly exciting.

Tools to Invest In (if you haven't yet)

 Food scale

 Candy Thermometer

 Molcajete

 dough scraper

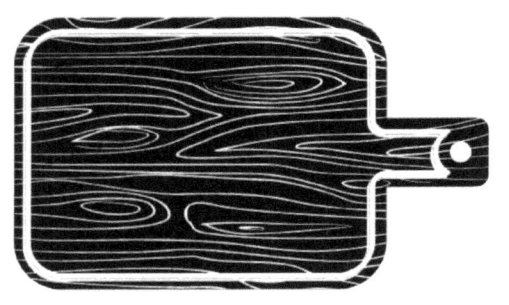 Butcher Block

 A good set of knives

 Dutch Oven

 Really sharp Vegetable Peeler

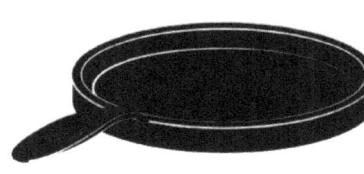 Seasoned Cast Iron Skillets, Different sizes

 Stoneware Plates

 Meat Thermometer

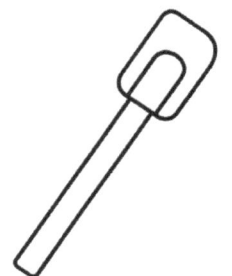 Silicone spatulas

 Heavy-Duty stand mixer

KITCHEN CONVERSION CHART

LIQUID MEASURES

CUPS	QUARTS	PINTS	GALLONS	FLUID OZ
16 cup	4 qt	8 pt	1 gal	128 fl oz
8 cup	2 qt	4 pt	1/2 gal	64 fl oz
4 cup	1 qt	2 pt	1/4 gal	32 fl oz
2 cup	1/2 qt	1 pt	1/8 gal	16 fl oz
1 cup	1/4 qt	1/2 pt	1/16 gal	8 fl oz

DRY MEASURES

CUPS	OUNCES	TABLESPOONS	TEASPOONS	GRAMS
1 cup	8 oz	16 tbsp	48 tsp	229 g
3/4 cup	6 oz	12 tbsp	36 tsp	171 g
2/3 cup	5.4 oz	11 tbsp	32 tsp	152 g
1/2 cup	4 oz	8 tbsp	24 tsp	114 g
1/3 cup	2.7 oz	5 tbsp	16 tsp	76 g
1/4 cup	2 oz	4 tbsp	12 tsp	57 g
1/8 cup	1 oz	2 tbsp	6 tsp	29 g
1/16 cup	0.5 oz	1 tbsp	3 tsp	14 g

TEMPERATURE
CONVERSION CHART

OVEN TEMPERATURES

	SLOW				MODERATE				HOT		
°F	225	250	275	300	325	350	375	400	425	450	475	500
°C	110	120	140	150	165	180	190	200	220	230	245	260
°C FAN	90	100	120	130	150	160	170	180	200	210	220	240
GAS MARK	1/4	1/2	1	2	3	4	5	6	7	8	9	10

COOKING TEMPERATURES

		Beef	Pork	Lamb	Chicken	Seafood
RARE	°F	125	/	/	/	/
	°C	52	/	/	/	/
MEDIUM RARE	°F	135	150	145	/	/
	°C	57	65	63	/	/
MEDIUM	°F	145	155	160	/	/
	°C	63	68	71	/	/
MEDIUM WELL	°F	150	160	165	/	/
	°C	65	71	74	/	/
WELL DONE	°F	160	160	170	165	145
	°C	71	71	77	74	63

Get in on This
Appetizers

The first recipe in this book is the first thing I ever made as a newlywed in my early 20's that my family really loved and started asking me to cook more often. I had had something similar to this at Cheesecake Factory years ago and wanted to see if I could make it myself. I still think of it as my only true specialty because everyone asks me to make it so much. It is a little bit of prep but a lot of reward.

Desert Honey

Fire Grilled Artichokes with Aioli

Serves 4

Ingredients:

- Two large artichokes, prepped
- ½ Cup of Mayonnaise
- 2 Tablespoons of Lemon Juice
- 1 clove of minced garlic
- Salt and pepper to taste
- Extra Virgin Olive Oil

For the aioli: Mix all aioli ingredients in a small bowl and set aside.
Prepare your steamer basket. Fill a saucepan about halfway with water and place it over high heat. Set the steamer basket on top of the saucepan and cover the basket with a lid. Let the water come to a boil while you prep the artichoke.

The first step is to properly prep the artichoke before steaming them.
Using scissors, clip the sharp points off the artichoke leaves.
With a large chef's knife, carefully slice the artichoke in half. Using a paring knife, carefully carve out the furry matter in the choke and remove the purple leaves as they are inedible.

Place 2 artichoke halves at a time in the steamer basket and let them steam for 7-10 minutes or until the stem is fork-tender.

Drizzle the artichoke halves with olive oil and a sprinkle of salt. Place them cut-side down on a hot grill or a cast iron skillet and cook for about two minutes until you have them charred to your liking.
Sprinkle with a touch more salt and olive oil. Serve immediately.

5 | Desert Honey

"Baby Crackers" and Caviar with French Shallot Mousse

This little snack is a sweet memory for my dad and sister. My dad would come home late at night from working retail hours and find my sister awake waiting for him. As a special snack, my dad would pick up Gerber baby crackers on the way home from work and a jar of caviar. Bowfin caviar or Black Lumpfish is a less expensive alternative to the ultra-high-end Beluga caviar and has that super tart saltiness of black caviar that I crave so much. Salmon roe is also excellent! I recommend giving this a try if you want to take your snack game to impressive heights! Don't we all?!

Ingredients:

- Bowfin or Black Lumpfish Caviar, or salmon roe
- Unsalted Crackers

For the shallot mousse:
- 8 oz of shallots, peeled and boiled
- 1/3 cup of heavy whipping cream
- Fine salt and pepper to taste

Fill a medium sized saucepan with water and bring to a boil. Peel the shallots and add them to the boiling water. Cook until they are soft and translucent.
Put the shallots in a food processor and process until they are puréed.
Pass the puréed shallots through a fine mesh sieve into a bowl and set aside.
Pour heavy whipping cream in to the bowl of a standmixer and whip until it reaches stiff peaks. Fold the shallot purée into the whipped cream and season with salt and pepper.

Spoon a dollop of shallot mouse onto a cracker and top with caviar. Serve immediately.

Blue Corn Fried Okra

I have fond memories of visiting my grandmother in North Carolina and arriving there late at night after a very long and weary road trip with my older siblings. As a late-night snack, she would fry okra this way as many southerners do with this particular staple. People seem to love or hate okra and there's no in-between. I for one love the slimy texture with plenty of salt. My grandmother only used flour for breading, but it is common to use cornmeal instead. In my version, I use blue cornmeal instead of yellow corn for the stone-ground texture and it adds something extra.

Serves 3

Ingredients:

1 lb. of fresh okra sliced into 1" pieces
¼ cup of all-purpose flour
¼ cup of Maseca Azul (Blue Cornmeal)
½ Coarse Salt
¼ Cup of Vegetable Oil for frying

Toss the fresh okra in both flours and salt. Add the vegetable oil to a cast-iron skillet and heat to medium-high heat. Put the breaded okra in the pan and fry until golden brown. Serve immediately.

Bratwurst in Puff Pastry with Smokey Ketchup and Honey Mustard

This is an easy, tailgating-style appetizer idea that was inspired by a Martha Stewart recipe I saw years ago. It is super tasty and even better if you customize your own dipping sauces.

Serves 6

Ingredients:

- 4 good bratwursts, store- bought
- 1 sheet of puff pastry, thawed
- Poppy seeds
- Heavy cream for brushing the pastry

For the Smokey Ketchup Sauce
- ¼ cup of ketchup
- ¼ cup of Worcestershire sauce
- 1 teaspoon of brown sugar

Combine ingredients in a small bowl and set aside.

For the Honey Mustard
- 1/3 cup of Dijon Mustard
- ¼ cup of raw unfiltered Desert Honey
- ¼ cup of Mayonnaise
- 1 tablespoon of lemon juice

How to make it:

Preheat the oven to 425 degrees. Heat a cast iron skillet to medium-high heat. Place the bratwurst in a skillet and poke a few holes in each with a fork. Cook the bratwurst to recommended temperature on package instructions.

Sprinkle flour on a work surface and roll out puff pastry in a 14x16 rectangle. Using a very sharp knife or pizza cutter, cut puff pastry into large 4 triangle patterns. Using a fork, poke a few holes in each triangle.

Wrap each sausage in puff pastry dough and brush with heavy cream. Sprinkle poppy seeds.

Bake for 20-25 minutes until the pastry is golden brown. Let it cool and slice in diagonal pieces. Serve with dipping sauces.

Giant California Roll

The giant California roll is an epic appetizer that was served at a restaurant and brewery here called Yardhouse. We used to specifically go for it, but they sadly took it off the menu. The good news is that this simplified version is not difficult to make at home and doesn't require sushi-making skills or special equipment. It is, however, a little pricey if you choose to use Masago. But it is well worth it for a night in or a special occasion.

Ingredients:
- 8 sticks of imitation crab, finely minced
- ¼ cup of mayonnaise
- ¼ teaspoon of salt
- 1 ½ cups of sushi rice (page 60)
- 1 small cucumber, julienned
- 1 large sheet of seaweed cut into squares and an extra piece sliced into strips as a garnish
- 1 avocado, sliced
- ½ teaspoon of sesame seeds
- Masago

First, find the mold that you would like to use to shape your California roll. A plastic tupperware bowl works perfectly as a mold. Mine is approximately 6" across and about 3" deep. The first step is to make the crab mix. Pulse the imitation crab in a food processor with the mayonnaise and salt. Add a little more mayonnaise if the mix appears dry. It should be somewhat creamy in consistency as it will be easier to shape

Prepare the bowl or mold by lining it with plastic wrap with a few inches of overhang. Take the crab mixture and pack it down as the first layer in the bowl. Add the julienned pieces of cucumber and press lightly. Add the slices of avocado, but reserve a few for garnish. Cover this layer with the square-cut pieces of seaweed. Lastly, add the sushi rice and pack it into a thick layer that reaches the top of the mold. Chill the mold in the refrigerator for about 30 minutes.

After the mold has chilled, place a plate over the top of the mold. Flip the plate over so that the sushi slides easily out of the mold. Then gently remove the plastic wrap. Spread the desired amount of Masago on the top layer. Garnish with the sliced pieces of seaweed, a fan of avocado, and cucumber chunks. Top with sesame seeds and drizzle soy sauce around the base. Serve immediately. Store leftovers in an airtight container up to a day.

Fried Panela with Herbs

There are some who can resist sizzling fried cheese and while I admire their resolve, I am not one of those people. Fried panela is so easy and works wonders as a last minute appetizer when you are entertaining. The olive oil herb dressing gets drizzled on the top at the end with a squeeze of lime making a perfect bite of gooey, salty, and tangy bliss.

Serves 3-4

Ingredients:

- 10 oz. of Panela Basket Cheese
- ¼ cup of extra virgin olive oil
- ½ teaspoon of fresh thyme, finely minced
- ½ teaspoon of fresh parsley, finely minced
- ¼ teaspoon of dried oregano
- 1/8 teaspoon of crushed red pepper
- ½ teaspoon of pink Himalayan salt
- ¼ teaspoon of white pepper
- A Squeeze of lime juice

Combine the olive oil with herbs and seasonings in a small bowl. Drizzle some olive oil in a cast iron skillet and heat to medium-high heat. Place the cheese on the hot pan and fry for 1-2 minutes until dark brown on both sides and soft in the middle. Remove from heat and pour olive oil mixture on top of the fried cheese round. Serve it sizzling in a hot skillet immediately with chips.

Simple Heirloom Tomato Salad

This simple Heirloom tomato salad is a perfect side for meals in the hot summer. My brother is very health conscious, and everything he cooks is fresh and simple This is one of my favorite things he makes because it's light but also satisfying. This salad is a perfect side for a delicate grilled fish or even as the layers of a toasted tomato sandwich.

Serves 2-3

- 4 large heirloom tomatoes
- 2 Tablespoons of Extra Virgin Olive Oil
- 2 tablespoons of apple cider vinegar
- Pink Himalayan salt to taste
- Freshly cracked black pepper

Slice heirloom tomatoes into thick, steak-like slices. Arrange them on a large flat serving plate.
In a small bowl, whisk together olive oil, apple cider vinegar, salt, and pepper. Pour over prepared tomatoes. Chill briefly before serving

Laura's Crispy

My mother-in-law makes this super crispy, super tasty little tostada-like snack that is so good; we eat them as soon as they come out of the frying pan! They are very simple but most definitely a crowd-pleaser.

Corn Tortillas
- Shredded Mexican Cheese Blend
- Salt
- ¼ cup of vegetable oil for frying

Heat the vegetable oil in a skillet until it begins smoking. Add 3 corn tortillas and allow them to fry until they form dark spots such that when they are lifted out of the pan, they do not flop but hold their shape. This can take a few minutes to reach this level of crispiness.

As soon as the tortilla comes out of the fryer, salt it with about 3 strong shakes of a saltshaker. Top with cheese and allow it to melt for a minute or so. Repeat with the next batches.

Pimento Cheese

Pimento cheese is the epitome of classic Southern spreadable goodness. The recipe is so simple, it will barely entertain you but it can literally go on anything. A lot of restaurants in the south serve it on burgers, on fried chicken sandwiches or as a grilled cheese. There are a lot of different versions out there that add all kinds of different ingredients to spice it up. My family keeps it super simple, and I feel like I will get in trouble if I change it, but the possibilities are endless.

Serves 4-6

Ingredients:

- 8 oz. block of sharp cheddar cheese, grated
- A heaping half cup of mayonnaise, preferably Duke's Mayonnaise
- 1 (4 oz.) jar of sliced pimentos
- A pinch of salt

Grate the whole block of cheddar cheese. Mix in mayonnaise and pimentos and a pinch of salt. Serve with saltines.

Tip: You can prepare pimento cheese and refrigerate it up to 3 days before serving.

Blistered Shishito Peppers with Flaky Sea Salt

Shishito peppers are small green peppers in the 'sweet chili pepper' variety. They are usually mild, but if you get a spicy one, it's considered good luck! My mother-in-law traveled to Spain, and these were served in some of the tapas places she visited there. She made them when she got back from her trip, and I fell in love. They are one of my favorite snacks ever and so easy to prepare. All you need to do is season them and blister them on high heat and voila! It's party time.

Serves 4-6

Ingredients:

- 12 oz. of shishito peppers, washed and thoroughly patted dry.
- Extra Virgin Olive Oil, preferably cold-pressed.
- Flaky sea salt.

Drizzle olive oil over the peppers and sprinkle with about ½ Teaspoon of flaky sea salt, tossing together in a bowl. Heat a cast iron skillet to high heat. Carefully add peppers to the hot skillet, but have a lid ready as the oil will pop. Once blistered on all sides, turn off the heat. Serve in a skillet after letting them cool off for a for a few minutes.

Tapas bar in Barcelona taken by Laura

Spam Musubi

Spam Musubi originates all the way back to World War II, but I did not get to experience it until about 7 years ago when I was a student in nursing school. It is a simple roll of fried spam wrapped in Nori (or seaweed) with a thick layer of sushi rice. Enjoy dipped in sweet teriyaki sauce or with soy sauce and you may crave it all the time as I do.

Serves 4-6

Ingredients:

- 1 can of Spam, cut into slices
- 1 cup of sushi rice (page 60)
- 1 package of Nori or sushi-grade seaweed paper
- Teriyaki sauce

Fry individual slices of spam until just golden brown on each side and set aside. Press ¼ cup of rice onto the far edge of the nori and form a rectangle. Drizzle a small amount of sauce onto the rice and place a piece of fried Spam on top. Roll the seaweed over the rice and Spam (like you would a burrito) and use a touch of water to seal the edge. Slice the roll in half and serve immediately or wrap in plastic wrap to store.

Steamed Pork Dumplings

Yummy and perfect dumplings every time for dim sum nights

Ingredients:

- 1 lb. of ground pork
- 4 cloves of minced garlic
- 3 stalks of scallions, thinly sliced
- 2 tablespoons of hoisin sauce
- 1 teaspoon of black sesame oil
- ½ teaspoon of fresh ginger, finely minced
- Kosher salt
- Black pepper
- 24 square dumpling wrappers

In a large mixing bowl, combine ground pork, garlic, scallions, hoisin sauce, sesame oil, ginger, salt, and pepper. Mix until well combined and set aside.
Prepare a small bowl filled with water and lay out your first wonton wrapper. Dip your finger in the water and trace the edge of the wonton paper to wet it. This will help the wontons stick together when you shape them.
Scoop a tablespoon of filling and place it in the center of the wonton. Fold the bottom edge to the top edge to seal. If you have a dumpling press, you can place the dumpling in it with the sealed edge facing out and press down to form the crimped edge. Alternatively, you can trim the excess from the edges with a knife and crimp the edges using a fork.

Prepare a steamer pot or bamboo steamer over a burner at medium-high heat. Line the steamer with parchment paper to prevent the dumplings from sticking.

Place the dumplings in the steamer basket and cover. Steam for about 15 minutes. Transfer them to a plate and garnish with sesame seeds. Use Ponzu or soy sauce on the side for dipping. Serve immediately.

Rainbow Carrot and Whipped Feta Tart with Orange Blossom Honey

This is a very tasty, and very colorful appetizer that works for any gathering throughout the seasons as rainbow carrots are available year-round. The roasted carrots with the salty feta whip finished with a honey drizzle is just simply meant to be.

Serves 6-8

Ingredients:
- 1 sheet of puff pastry
- 6 large rainbow carrots
- 3 oz. of feta cheese
- 1 head of roasted garlic
- 6 oz. of whipped cream cheese, softened
- Salt and pepper
- Orange Blossom Honey for drizzle

Preheat the oven to 400 degrees. Take a fresh head of garlic and slice off the top. Place in a square sheet of aluminum foil and drizzle olive oil on top and sprinkle with salt. Wrap the garlic in foil and roast for about an hour. When done, remove foil and squeeze the soft roasted garlic into a small bow.

In a medium bowl, mix together cream cheese and feta cheese vigorously until smooth. Add the roasted garlic along with salt and pepper to taste. Mix thoroughly to combine and set aside.

Peel and slice rainbow carrots on the bias (diagonally)into 1/4 inch thick slices. Prepare a steamer basket and steam carrots for about 10 minutes until tender, but still al dente. Prepare a large baking sheet and line it with parchment paper. Take a sheet of thawed puff pastry and sprinkle flour on top. Roll out the puff pastry into a 14 x 16 rectangle. Using a fork, poke several holes into the puff pastry. This will help it release large air pockets when baking. Spread the cheese over the puff pastry, leaving about a one-inch border. Arrange the steamed carrots on top in a succession pattern. Place the sheet pan in the oven and bake for about 20 minutes until puff pastry is golden brown. After baking, drizzle a thin stream of orange blossom honey all over or as much as desired. Serve immediately.

29 | Desert Honey

Main Courses and Some Things on the Side

Amy's Lazy Braciola

Amy: this recipe isn't a traditional braciola, but it is a way to achieve the low and slow flavors of the Southern Italian classic on a weeknight. The sauce makes a delicious velvety tomato gravy and the roast is incredibly tender. Serve top of parmesan mashed potatoes or your favorite pasta noodles and you will have the makings of a savory slow braise without as much effort.

Serves 8   Cook time: 8 hours

Ingredients:

- 3 lb. of Chuck Roast or larger if available
- 2 ½ teaspoons of coarse salt
- 1 ½ teaspoons of cracked pepper
- 2 teaspoons of dried oregano
- 2 jars of Rao's marinara sauce
- 15 oz. can of diced tomatoes
- 3 cloves of minced garlic
- ½ cup of freshly grated parmesan cheese
- ½ cup of freshly grated mozzarella cheese
- Italian Breadcrumbs for topping (optional)
- Sliced pancetta for topping (optional)

Season the chuck roast generously with salt and pepper and place in a slow cooker. Add the dried oregano and pour in two jars of Rao's marinara sauce, and the can of diced tomatoes. Add the garlic cloves and both cheeses.

Set the slow cooker to the high setting and cook for about 8 hours or until the roast is very fork-tender. Ladle over a spread of parmesan mashed potatoes. Top with
additional parmesan and pancetta if available.

Parmesan Mashed Potatoes

I have to warn you about this recipe. Don't make these mashed potatoes unless you want to be elected the person who will always have to bring the mashed potatoes to every function from now on. They are so decadent and deliciously cheesy that, at first, you may think that you are looking at a fondue, but it is, in fact, mashed potatoes. A whole five ounces of parmesan cheese with the heavy cream creates the stretchy-gooey-creamy consistency. This is a side that can really end up stealing the show.

Serves 4-6

Ingredients

- 2 ½ lbs. of peeled and boiled Russet potatoes
- 1 ½ cups of heavy whipping cream
- 1 teaspoon of kosher salt
- ½ Stick of unsalted butter
- 5 oz. of parmesan cheese
- A handful of shredded mozzarella cheese

In a large pot of salted boiling water, add peeled russet potatoes and cook until fork-tender. Strain and transfer the potatoes to a large saucepan and, over low heat, add cream, butter, salt, and cheeses. Using a hand mixer (or potato masher), mash the potatoes until the mixture is creamy and well combined. Stir them on low heat until all the cheese is melted. You may add more cream and cheese if needed to achieve the cheese-pull consistency. Serve immediately.

Bean and Bacon Soup with Pimento Grilled Cheese

This is a menu special at Mayberry's, which is an ice cream parlor and diner in High Point, North Carolina. Bean and bacon soup is a rich and creamy soup, and a favorite in the south. This recipe is a good way to get you out of a soup rut, as I don't see it served all that often anymore, but it is very delicious. Serve it along side a pimento grilled cheese sandwich and enjoy some time in soup-and-sandwich heaven.

Serves 8-10   Cook time: 1 hour

Ingredients

Serves 8-10   Cook time: 1 hour

- 10 strips of bacon, chopped.
- 3 celery stalks, diced
- 3 carrots, diced
- ½ of a yellow onion, diced
- 2 cloves of chopped garlic
- Two 16 oz. cans of pinto beans
- Two 16 oz. cans of chicken broth
- 1 bay leaf
- One 4 oz. can of tomato sauce

In a heavy-bottomed stockpot or Dutch oven, fry the chopped bacon until crispy. Spoon out the bacon and let it drain on a paper towel, but leave about 2 tablespoons of bacon fat in the pot. Add the chopped celery, carrots, onion, and garlic and cook for a few minutes until the pieces become soft and the onions are translucent. Add the canned beans with all the liquid and the two cans of chicken broth. Add the bay leaf. Bring to a boil and reduce the heat to let the soup simmer for about an hour.

Using an immersion blender, blend the soup until it reaches a smooth consistency. Alternatively, you could transfer the soup to a blender if you don't have an immersion blender.
Add the can of tomato sauce and stir it in to combine. Lastly, add the cooked bacon back to the pot and serve. (con't)

Grilled Pimento Cheese Sandwich

- Two slices of white bread
- ¼ cup of pimento cheese
- Mayonnaise

Heat a cast iron skillet to high heat. Spread mayonnaise on both bread slices and lay the mayo side down on the hot skillet. This is an old restaurant trick that will toast the bread to a deep golden brown. Drop spoonfuls of the pimento cheese on to the bread and flip one piece over on top of the other. Press down and cook until cheese is melted. Serve immediately.

Mayberry is famous for this gigantic sundae called the Lock, Stock & Barrel. I've never ordered it but it's only a matter of time.

Braised Short Rib

Ingredients:

- 4-5 lbs. of Beef Short Ribs (I used Bone-in)
- Kosher salt
- Black pepper
- Neutral Oil, such as canola
- 1 chopped onion
- 2 sticks of celery, chopped
- 2 carrots, chopped
- 2 cloves of minced garlic
- 1 cup of balsamic vinegar
- 1 cup of red wine or red wine vinegar
- 2 quarts of low-sodium chicken broth
- 1/4 cup of jarred horse-radish
- 2 handfuls of flat-leaf parsley, chopped

Coat a large, heavy Dutch oven with oil. Season the short ribs generously with salt. When the oil begins to smoke, add half of the short ribs. Brown the tops, bottoms, and sides of each short rib. Transfer to a plate and start the next batch. Take time to really let things brown; about 30 minutes.
Remove the ribs from the Dutch oven and add the carrots, onion, celery, and garlic.
Stir until onions become translucent and then add the balsamic vinegar and red wine. Turn the burner up to high and let the liquid reduce down by about half.
Pour in the chicken stock. Add horseradish and fresh parsley. Put the short ribs back in the pot. Cover and reduce the heat to low on the burner. Let it braise for about 3 1/2 hours. If needed, you can preheat your oven to 300 degrees and let the ribs braise in the oven.

When the short ribs are done, they will slide off the bone or will have already separated from the bone. That means it's perfect. If the ribs are still sticking to the bone and the meat doesn't fall apart easily, let it go longer.

Remove the ribs from the liquid and strain the vegetables from the braising liquid. You can reserve the liquid and make a gravy (delicious) or store the leftover meat in it so that it doesn't dry out in the fridge.

Desert Honey

Easy Pasta Carbonara

Pasta Carbonara is one of those back-pocket recipes that is easy to make on the weeknight and is sure to please. It is relatively easy to make this luxurious pasta and as long as you have bacon, eggs, parmesan cheese, and pasta on hand you are golden. Pancetta is preferred but if you have bacon instead, it is totally acceptable in my book.

Serves 4

Ingredients:

- 10 slices of thick cut bacon or pancetta chopped
- 12 oz. of spaghetti noodles
- 2 cloves of minced garlic
- 2 large eggs and 2 large egg yolks
- 1 oz. (1/3 cup) of grated Pecorino Romano cheese
- 1 oz. (1/3 cup) of grated Parmesan cheese
- Salt
- Black Pepper
- Chopped Italian Parsley for garnish

Heat a large pot of water to boiling and add a generous amount of salt. Cook the spaghetti noodles for about 1 minute less than package instructions. Be sure to reserve about 1 to 1 ½ cups of pasta water.

In a separate bowl, mix the eggs, both cheeses, ¼ teaspoon of salt, and ¼ teaspoon of black pepper and set aside.

In a large sauté pan, cook the chopped bacon until almost crispy. Spoon out the bacon onto a plate to drain, leaving about 2 tablespoons of bacon fat in the pan. Add the minced garlic and cook until fragrant.

Turn the heat down to medium-low and add the spaghetti noodles to the sauté pan. Toss the noodles with tongs to coat. Add back the bacon and pour in the bowl of the egg and cheese mix. Toss a few more times to coat and add a cup of pasta water. Continue to stir the pasta until a creamy sauce forms. Add the rest of the pasta water if needed to thin out the sauce. Grate Pecorino and Parmesan on top, sprinkle with parsley and serve.

Chicken Katsu— Beijing Noodle Style

One of my favorite Chinese restaurants here in Las Vegas is Beijing Noodle house in Caesars Palace. If you are planning a Vegas vacation, it is a must-try! Their menu is amazing and their noodle options are endless. One of my favaorites on the menu is their Chicken Katsu. I was craving it, so I threw together a simple recipe and paired it with "perfect sushi rice" (page 60) on the side. This recipe comes together pretty quickly, so it's totally doable on a school night.

6 servings

Ingredients:
- 6 boneless, skinless chicken thighs
- ½ Box of Panko Breadcrumbs
- 3 eggs, beaten in a bowl
- ½ Cup of water
- 1 ½ Cups of All-purpose flour.
- Vegetable oil for frying
- Kosher Salt
- Black Pepper
- Katsu Sauce for dipping (A1 steak sauce and Ketchup)

Add ½ cup of vegetable oil to a cast iron skillet, set the heat to medium-low. Prepare 3 separate bowls. In the first bowl, crack 3 eggs and beat lightly. Add about half a cup of water to the eggs. In the second bowl, add flour with about ½ tablespoon of kosher salt and ½ teaspoon of black pepper and stir to incorporate. In the third bowl, mix the Panko breadcrumbs with 2 teaspoons of kosher salt and toss to combine.

Using tongs, dip the chicken thigh in the egg and water mixture. Next, dredge the chicken in flour mix and coat thoroughly. Dip once again in egg and water. Lastly, dredge in breadcrumbs and coat thoroughly. Repeat for the remaining pieces, placing each one on a plate until you're ready to fry.

Increase the heat of the frying pan to medium. Work in batches, adding no more than 2-3 thighs at a time so that you do not overcrowd the pan. Fry each side for about 2 minutes at a time, placing a sheet of foil on top while frying. Check the temperature with a meat thermometer to ensure that the internal temperature is at least 160 degrees in the thickest part of the meat. Transfer to a cooling rack to drain.

Allow the chicken to cool slightly and slice on the bias. Drizzle with sauce and serve immediately.

Desert Honey

Lighter Eggplant Parmesan

Eggplant parmesan is a classic and easy favorite that is satisfying and also vegetarian. I make a lightened-up version that skips the frying and instead bakes the eggplant slices, which also saves the extra work. The cheese is saved only for the top layer, which cuts back on the calories as well and makes it a little healthier. Lighter, yes a little, but just as great as the original.

Ingredients:
- Two medium-sized eggplants
- 3 egg whites
- ½ cup of water
- 2 cups of Panko breadcrumbs or Italian breadcrumbs
- 1 cup of freshly grated parmesan cheese
- 1 28 oz. jar of good marinara sauce, such as Rao's
- 1 teaspoon of Salt
- 1 teaspoon of pepper
- Italian parsley for garnish

Preheat the oven to 400 degrees.
Begin by slicing the eggplants into thick slices. Prepare a parchment-lined baking sheet. In a separate bowl, whisk together the egg whites and water. In another bowl, pour about two cups of Panko breadcrumbs and season with salt and pepper.
Take a slice of eggplant and dunk it into the water and egg white mixture. Then dredge it in the breadcrumbs and lay flat on the baking sheet. Repeat for the remaining slices.
Bake the eggplant for about 30 minutes or until golden brown.
While the eggplant is baking, spray a 9" x 11" baking dish with cooking spray.
Take the eggplant slices out of the oven and arrange the first layer in the baking dish.
Spread a layer of sauce and repeat for the remaining slices.
Sprinkle parmesan cheese on the top layer and bake for about 45 minutes or until it starts bubbling. Allow it to cool and then sprinkle on Italian parsley for garnish.

Elote Cornbread and Abarriata Chili

If you've roped yourself into a chili cook-off and need an idea, I got you right here. Elote cornbread as a concept came to me out of nowhere and I had to make it a thing. I have no idea if it is already a thing or not. I did not Google it beforehand. I'm sure I am not the first to think of it. This isn't just any cornbread, and the texture was very tender and moist. I love a good honey and butter combo, but this was a fun twist and has earned a spot as a permanent go-to in my recipe book. Abarriata means "angry" in Italian and refers to a spicy tomato-based pasta sauce, much like Marinara. It has a smooth heat from crushed red pepper, but I cut through the heat a little bit with a splash of whole milk (for the kids). Totally optional to leave it out and keep it as-is if you prefer the heat.

Serves 8 Cooktime: 3 hours

Batter for the cornbread:
- 1 can of Sweet corn
- 1¼ Cup of All-Purpose flour
- ¾ Cups of Corn Meal
- ¼ Cup of sugar
- 2 Teaspoons of baking powder
- ½ Teaspoon of Salt
- 1 Cup of whole milk
- 2 Eggs (Beaten)
- 5 oz. of Queso Fresco, crumbled

Elote Spread Ingredients:
- ¼ cup of mayonnaise
- ¼ of sour cream
- 2 Tablespoons of Mexican Crema
- ¼ tsp of kosher salt
- Black pepper
- 1 Teaspoon of Paprika
- ¼ Teaspoon of Cayenne
- 1 Tablespoon of Lime juice
- Queso fresco, crumbled
- 1 Tablespoon of chopped Cilantro.
- Combine in a small bowl.

Preheat Oven to 400 Degrees
Cook the canned sweet corn in cast iron skillet or frying pan on high heat until the corn is charred. Be sure to cover with foil while cooking because kernels will pop and fly out.
Prepare the Elote spread and put it in a bowl to the side.
Add all batter ingredients to a bowl and mix until combined.
Fold in charred corn and Queso fresco.
Generously spray a 10" skillet with non-stick baking spray or grease thoroughly.
Pour batter into the skillet.
Dollop spoonfuls of Elote spread on top of the batter. Take a toothpick or a very sharp knife and swirl the tops. The trick to a nice swirl is to only dip the tip of the toothpick in about a centimeter. If you dip it any more than that, the dollops will just mix and you won't get the nice design. Good tip if you're making a marble cake or something like that.
Bake for 30 minutes. Tap your fingers on the top of the cornbread. If it is solid and

bouncy, it's done. If it indents slightly, continue baking in 3-minute intervals. You could always insert a toothpick. But if you don't want to poke holes in your bread or cakes, this is a nice baking skill to master. Sprinkle the remaining Queso and cilantro on top to garnish.

Arrabbiata Chili:
• 1lb. of Ground Beef
• 1 Sweet Onion, chopped
• 2 Cloves of smashed Garlic
• 2 Tablespoons of tomato paste
• Salt and pepper to taste
• 2 Red Bell peppers, seeds removed and chopped into pieces.
• 1 large carrot, diced
• 2 jars of Arrabbiata sauce
• 1-2 Cup of water. Add gradually to desired consistency.
• ¼ Cup of Cornmeal
• Worcestershire sauce. Several dashes.
• Soy sauce. Also several dashes
• 1 Can of pinto beans (if desired). I do desire; however, keep in mind that it will increase the thickness of the chili significantly. Not a bad thing; just add water to thin it out.
• Splash of whole milk
• Salt and Pepper

Add 1 Tablespoon of butter to a skillet.
Sauté onions with smashed garlic.
Add tomato paste and ground beef and cook until browned. Add salt and pepper to taste.
Add to a Dutch oven (or a slow cooker) bell pepper, carrot, Arrabbiata sauce, water, cornmeal, and Worcestershire and soy sauce.
Add in meat and onion mixture. If using a Dutch oven, simmer on stovetop over low heat for about 2 hours.

Add a splash of milk. Taste and add salt and pepper. Add a can of pinto beans (drained) about 10-15 minutes before serving. If using a slow cooker, cook on the low setting for about 6 hours and add beans just before serving.

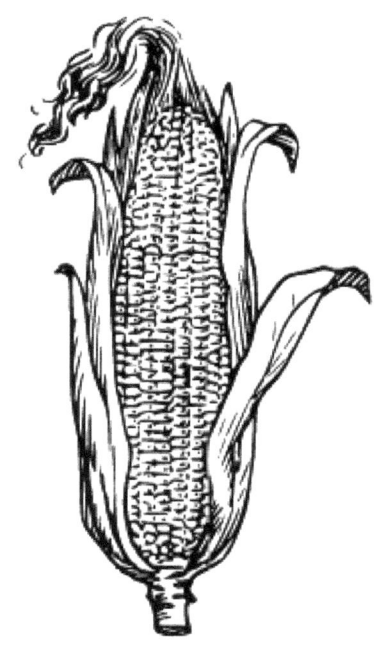

Escargot

Escargot is just pure romance, like all things French. My bestie Desi and I went to a French restaurant one night in L.A. and we had one of the best meals of our lives. Everything we had was phenomenal, but the escargot was an experience. C'est magnifique! Escargot is actually very simple to make and incredibly delicious. The snails and shells are typically sold in specialty fine food grocery stores or online, but they are relatively inexpensive, and the shells can be reused if cleaned and stored properly. It can also be made a day ahead, which is great to know if you like to entertain.

Serves 4-6 Cook time: 45 minutes

Ingredients:

- 1 cup (2 sticks) of European-style butter, room temperature
- 1 tablespoon of dry white wine
- 1 ½ teaspoons of kosher salt
- 1 ½ teaspoon of freshly ground black pepper
- 12 garlic cloves, very finely chopped
- 1 large shallot, finely chopped
- ¾ cup of finely chopped parsley
- 24 large empty escargots shells
- 24 extra-large canned escargots

Preheat the oven to 450 degrees. Beat softened butter in a bowl until smooth. Add wine and salt and resume beating until incorporated. Add garlic, shallot, and parsley and mix until incorporated. Scoop the butter mixture into a pastry bag with a fitted tip, or alternatively, a zip lock bag with the corner snipped off. Tuck a snail into a shell and pipe the butter mixture inside to cap it off. Repeat with the remaining snails. Arrange the snails in a baking dish or a large skillet and cook in the oven for about 10-15 minutes or until the butter starts bubbling. Enjoy with bread to soak up the gorgeous butter sauce.

Filipino Hot Dogs with Chili Crisp

Filipino Hot Dogs are one of my earliest food memories. We had moved to Troy Michigan one year when I was about 7 years old for a short period of time. We shared a duplex next door to a multigenerational Filipino family that had two children—a brother and a sister—who I played with almost every day. They were my best friends at the time and made the adjustment to moving to a new town a little bit easier. Almost every day for lunch, their father would make Filipino hot dogs and would invite me to join. I remember looking at the hot dogs and thinking "why are they so pink?" and being hesitant to try them. But once I did, I realized they were delicious (similar to Nathan's hot dogs) and every time I smelled them cooking, I would invite myself over. They are traditionally served as a breakfast item, as a sausage component, along with fried eggs and rice, or on a skewer. My favorite way to enjoy them is with a side of spicy chili crisp, which I find easily in Asian markets.

Ingredients:

- 1 pack of Filipino Hot Dogs with Cheese
- 1 teaspoon of Spicy Chili Crunch. I prefer the LaoGanMa brand
- Optional sides: Sushi rice with furikake seasoning, 2 oil fried eggs

Take a sharp knife and slice diagonal cuts through each hot dog about halfway through. Grill on high heat until charred. Spread a thin smear of chili crunch. Top Serve skewerd or with rice and fried eggs.

Fried egg method:
In a frying pan, add two tablespoons of cooking oil and heat until begins to smoke. Crack an egg on top of the oil, and while the egg is frying, tilt the pan to the side and spoon the oil from the bottom of the pan back on top of the eggs. Continue spooning hot oil over the egg until the top of it turns white. Set aside on a plate to cool and serve.

Desert Honey

Chorizo Dogs with Black Bean Whip

Ingredients:

- 4 chorizo sausages
- Homemade Flour tortillas (Page 97)
- 1 can of black beans
- 2 tablespoons of pork fat
- Pinch of cumin
- Grilled vegetables
- Cotija cheese

Cook the chorizo sausages on the grill until you have a nice char and the casing begins to burst.

Black Bean Whip:
In a saucepan, add the can of black beans with the liquid and bring to a simmer. Allow the beans to simmer for a few minutes until they begin to split. Add the pork fat and pinch of cumin. Whip the beans vigorously until you have a creamy whipped texture.

Spread the black bean whip on a flour tortilla. Top with sausage and grilled vegetables

Perfect Sushi Rice

Ingredients:

- 2 Cups of short grain sushi rice
- 2 1/2 Cups of water
- 2 Tablespoons of Rice Wine Vinegar
- 2 Tablespoons of white sugar
- 1 Tablespoon of salt.

The first step is to thoroughly wash your rice before cooking.
Pour rice in a mixing bowl and fill with water. Vigorously swish the rice around with your hand. Pour rice into a fine mesh strainer and pour the rice back into the mixing bowl. Repeat two more times until the water running off the rice is running clear. This will wash off excess starches from the rice that affect the texture in cooking.
Pour the rice and water into a sauce pan, or clay rice pot.
Stove top method: Bring rice and water to a boil. Turn heat to low and cover pot. Let the rice cook covered for about 15 minutes. If the rice looks dry at the end of steaming, add a small amount of water and stir.
Combine Vinegar, sugar and salt in a small, microwave safe bowl and set aside until rice is finished cooking.
Check doneness of rice after about 15 minutes. Turn off the heat and let the rice stand covered for 10 minutes.
 Heat the vinegar mixture in a microwave for about 1 minute. Salt and sugars should be about half dissolved. Pour the vinegar mixture into the rice and stir several times to ensure rice is coated. Serve immediately if using as a side or let cool if making sushi rolls.

Roast Chicken on Toast

Roast chicken is a dish that all home cooks should have in their back pocket. If you are new to cooking at home and have never made one yet, don't be intimidated! They are simple to cook and usually turn out delicious with little effort. If you've roasted many chickens in your day, this may add a new layer of flavor to your usual recipe. The trick is to roast your chicken in the oven with the chicken itself sitting on top of large pieces of bread. The bread will absorb the butter and juices while the chicken roasts, and will turn into an incredibly delicious crouton on the bottom of the pan. Everyone will fight over this part, so you're guaranteed to make it more than once.

Serves 4
Ingredients:

- 1 (5 pound) organic young chicken
- Coarse Salt
- Pepper
- 10 sprigs of fresh thyme
- 1 stick of butter (8 tablespoons), softened.
- 1 large yellow onion
- I head of garlic with top sliced off
- 1 lemon, cut in half
- 4 carrots, sliced in large pieces on the bias
- 4 Yukon Gold potatoes, cut into large chunks.
- 2 large pieces of bread. Optional to use white, wheat, sourdough.

Preheat oven to 425 degrees. Rinse off the top of the chicken and be sure to remove the neck and giblets that are typically stored in the cavity. These parts can be saved and frozen for future gravy and broth making. Pat the chicken thoroughly dry with paper towels and set aside.

Using a 9"x 13" inch baking dish, place the pieces of bread down that you are going to set the chicken on. Set the chicken on top of the bread. Season the chicken generously with coarse salt and pepper. Using your hands, slather the softened butter all over the chicken, covering the whole chicken as best as you can. Place the thyme, onion, and head of garlic, and lemon slices into the cavity of the chicken. Put the carrots and potatoes in the baking dish surrounding the chicken. Roast the chicken for about 1 hour and 30 minutes. The juices will run clear when it's done, but use a temperature probe and test many different areas of the chicken to register 165 degrees. When it is done cooking, let it rest covered in foil for about 30 minutes. Slice the chicken and serve with the vegetables and toast pieces on the side.

Mom's Chicken Divan

My mom's Chicken Divan recipe has a deliciously creamy sauce underneath a crispy layer of buttery breadcrumbs. When she makes it for us, it's hard to stay away from it, and there's hardly ever any leftover.

Serves 8

Ingredients:

- 2 Tablespoons of butter
- 3 Tablespoons of All-purpose flour
- 2 Teaspoons of chicken bouillon granules
- 2 Cups of milk
- ½ Cup of mayonnaise
- 2 packages (9 oz. each) of frozen broccoli spears, thawed and drained.
- 3 Cups of cubed, pre-cooked chicken breasts (or turkey)
- ½ Cup of grated medium cheddar cheese

For the topping:
- 1/3 Cup of plain breadcrumbs
- 1 Tablespoon of melted butter

Preheat the oven to 350 degrees. In a 2-quart saucepan, melt butter over medium-high heat. Add flour and bouillon granules. Stir and let the roux (the flour and butter mixture) cook for about a minute, or until it begins to bubble. Gradually pour in milk while whisking constantly. Turn off the heat and add mayonnaise and mustard.

Arrange broccoli spears in an ungreased 12"x 8" baking dish. Arrange cubes of chicken breast over the broccoli spears. Pour the sauce over the chicken and sprinkle the top with the grated cheese.

In a small bowl, mix the breadcrumbs and the melted butter. Sprinkle the breadcrumbs on top and bake for 30 minutes or until bubbly on top.

Mom's Clam Linguini

My mom is known to whip up late-night clam linguini for my dad, and after 40 years of marriage, I think she has pretty much perfected the art.

Serves 4-6
Ingredients:

- 12 oz. of linguine noodles
- 1 stick of butter (8 tablespoons)
- 1/3 cup of Extra Virgin Olive Oil
- 3/4 c. of chopped onions, yellow
- 2 cloves of fresh garlic, minced
- 1/4 tsp. of Old Bay Seasoning
- 2 16 oz. cans of Baby Clams (with liquid)

Cook linguine noodles according to package instructions. Drain noodles and set aside. In a large skillet, sauté onions in olive oil. Cook on medium-low heat until the onions are translucent. Add garlic, Old Bay, capers and clams (including liquid). Simmer for 8 minutes until the liquid reduces slightly. Pour over linguine top with grated Parmesan cheese

Janie's Rice

Another highly-requested recipe from my Aunt.

Serves 6-8
Ingredients:

- 1 Cup of Long-Grain White rice
- 2 cans of Campbell's chicken broth
- 2 cans of water
- 1 stick of butter
- A pinch of salt

Preheat the oven to 375 degrees. In a 9" x 13" casserole dish, pour in the rice and the cans of chicken broth, and two cans of water. Place the stick of butter in the middle. Sprinkle a pinch of salt on top. Bake until the rice has absorbed all the liquid and the top is very lightly browned, about 30-40 minutes. The consistency will be creamy; almost like a risotto. Serve immediately.

Janie's Southern Summer Squash Casserole

We request this dish from my Aunt Janie whenever we visit, and though she'd rather be shopping than be in the kitchen, she makes the most delicious comfort food. Her squash casserole is the squash casserole of your dreams; creamy, cheesey, and topped with crispy, bubbly goodnees. It's too good not to share and this recipe is perfect (and big enough) for just that. Enjoy, ya'll!

Serves 8-10
Ingredients:

- 6-8 yellow summer squash, sliced into ¼ inch thick
- 1 large white onion, roughly chopped
- 8 ounces of sour cream
- ½ a stick of butter (4 tablespoons)
- 2 cups of grated sharp cheddar cheese
- 1 15oz. can of cream of chicken soup
- ½ cup of plain panko breadcrumbs.
- 2 teaspoons of salt
- ½ a teaspoon of black pepper

For the topping:
- 1 cup of panko breadcrumbs
- 1 cup of grated sharp cheddar cheese

Preheat the oven to 400 degrees. Slice the squash into ¼ inch thick slices and chop up the onion into a large dice. Add the onion and the squash to a large pot of boiling water. Boil the squash and onion for 10 minutes and drain the liquid out. Transfer the squash and onions to a large mixing bowl. Add all other ingredients and mix until combined. Pour into an ungreased 9" x 13" inch casserole dish. In a separate bowl, mix the breadcrumbs and cheddar cheese. Sprinkle on the topping and bake for about 30-35 minutes until the top is brown and bubbling.

Shrimp and Grits

This shrimp and grits recipe is so like what I had in New Orleans one summer when my bestie and I took a girl's trip to New Orleans. We visited a restaurant called Muriel's, which is in one of the oldest buildings in the French Quarter. If you ever get a chance to visit Muriel's, you will notice that there is a nicely set table for the resident ghost and the spot itself is a main stop on the city's famous ghost tour. They are known for their crab cakes, but their shrimp and grits are also to die for. I don't think anyone could go wrong with a decadent shrimp and grits recipe, but this gets close to the greatness you may have if you go to The Big Easy itself.

Serves 8
Ingredients:

- 4 cups of water
- Salt
- 1 cup of stone-ground grits
- 2 cups of sharp cheddar cheese, shredded
- 6 tablespoons of butter
- 8 slices of thick-cut bacon
- 1 red bell pepper, seeds removed and diced
- 1 green bell pepper, seeds removed and diced
- 2 cloves of garlic, minced
- 1 pound of large shrimp, peeled and deveined
- 3 tablespoons of lemon juice
- 2 tablespoons of chopped parsley
- Pepper, to taste
- Cayenne, to taste

Cook the grits: Bring the water to a boil and add a teaspoon of salt. Pour in the grits and stir. Let the grits cook for about 20 minutes until all the water is absorbed. Once the grits are cooked, add the butter and cheese. Stir until it is creamy and melted together.

In a large skillet, fry the strips of bacon until crispy. Spoon out the bacon to drain on a paper towel, leaving about 2 tablespoons of fat in the skillet. Add the diced bell peppers and the minced garlic to the pan and let it cook in the bacon fat for a few minutes. Next, add the shrimp, lemon juice, parsley, a pinch of salt, a pinch of pepper, and a pinch of cayenne. Sauté for a few minutes until the shrimp turns pink.

Remove about half of the shrimp from the skillet and cut them into large pieces. Add the pieces of shrimp into the grits mixture and stir them in. Then spoon the grits into a baking dish or serving bowl and top with the rest of the shrimp mixture. Garnish with parsley and serve immediately.

Fried Chicken with Chinese Hot Mustard Vinaigrette

OK, so this fried chicken recipe isn't the shaggy crunchy breading that we all know and love, but you won't miss that here. This version is very crispy and incredibly tender. Once I tried this method, I could not get over it and I honestly haven't busted out a traditional breading in a while. This is inspired by one of my all-time favorite Chefs-David Chang and his amazing fried chicken recipe from Momofuku. My version is a little different and cuts some corners to speed up the process for busy-mom reasons and I created my own vinaigrette that gets drizzled on the hot crispy chicken at the end for a wow finish. There's never any leftovers and I think it's one of the best things I've ever made at home.

- A 3lb. Organic chicken broken down into 2 breasts, with wings 2 legs, 2 thighs
- ½ cup of sugar
- ½ cup of coarse salt
- 4 cups of vegetable oil for frying

Begin by patting the chicken quarters dry with a paper towel. Line a sheet pan with parchment paper and spread out the chicken pieces. Sprinkle the sugar on the dry skin in an even layer followed by the salt. Let the chicken sit in the refrigerator uncovered for 3-4 four hours. You can leave the chicken overnight at this point if you need to This will help dry out the skin and the dry rub will pull out moisture.

After 3-4 hours have passed, pull the chicken out and let it sit for about 30 minutes to take the chill off.

Prepare a steamer basket (I use a bamboo steamer basket) by filling a large pan or wok with water and heating it to a boil and placing the basket on top. The water level should not be so high that it touches the bottom section where the meat will lay. It is best practice to place the smaller pieces of meat (the legs) at the bottom while the larger pieces (breasts) on the top level. Cover the basket with the lid slightly offset and let the chicken steam for 35-40 minutes. Remove the chicken and place on a clean sheet pan. At this point, let it cool uncovered in the refrigerator for about an hour while you get the fryer set up.

Fill a large heavy bottomed pan or Dutch oven with oil and affix a thermometer to the side. Heat the oil to 375 degrees. Place the first batch of chicken in the oil and let it fry until deep golden brown which should take about 3 minutes per side. Once the chicken is golden brown and the internal temperature is at least 165 degrees, remove it from the oil and let it drain on a cooling rack. Repeat

these steps for the second batch. Once the chicken is cooked, pour on the Hot Mustard Vinaigrette.

Chinese Hot Mustard Vinaigrette

- 1/4 cup of champagne vinegar
- 1 Teaspoon of sugar
- 1 Teaspoon of salt
- 2-3 Tablespoons of Chinese Hot Mustard. Sun Luck is my preferred brand.
- 1/4 cup of Black Sesame Oil

Whisk all ingredients together and pour over fried chicken or have on the side.

Edemame Spaghetti with Cilantro Pesto

Desert Honey

Serves 4
Ingredients:

- 8 oz package of edamame spaghetti
- 1 cup of packed cilantro
- ½ cup of walnuts
- 1 large clove of garlic
- 1 picked Serrano pepper
- Juice of 1 lime
- ½ teaspoon of salt
- ¾ cup of cotija cheese
- ¾ cup of olive oil

Make the Cilantro Pesto: In a food processor, cilantro, walnuts, garlic, Serrano pepper, lime juice, salt, cotija cheese, and turn on to low speed. Slowly drizzle in olive oil until the pesto forms a whipped, creamy paste.

Cook the edamame spaghetti according to package instructions and drain. Drizzle some olive oil on the spaghetti and toss to coat. Add the pesto and toss the noodles to coat. Serve immediately or serve chilled.

Candy

Honey Smoked Spareribs

I hate to brag but this recipe is the best of its kind in its category. I've never had better ribs than this anywhere else. After studying the barbecue gods of YouTube like Malcom Reed and the great Aaron Franklin, we came up with an outstanding method for rib making that is so good that it has inspired a range of emotions amongst family members. The measurements in this recipe are not exact regarding the rub, because sometimes great things come from the heart. The idea is just a light, even coating of seasoning; whatever that means for the amount and size of ribs you're cooking. Unless the top of the shaker falls off while you're seasoning (it happens), you can't really mess it up.
 A Kamado-style grill is a ceramic dome-like type of grill. The Kamado (or ceramic cooker) style of grill that I own is a Green Egg, which is by far the biggest investment I've made in a home appliance, but it was well worth it since I am a lover of grilling. The Kamado ceramic grill is set up with 100% Natural Oak and Hickory Lump coals as opposed to briquettes. Charcoal briquettes are ignited using chemicals, whereas lump coals produce smoke from wood rather than a chemical reaction. These are important things to consider if you're just starting out. But I highly recommend watching the above-mentioned pros to begin your new passion.

Cook time: 5 hours.   Serves 4-6
- 3 lbs. of St. Louis Pork Spareribs (one full rack)
- Kinder's Seasoning: "The Blend" (Salt, Pepper, and Garlic)
- Holy Gospel BBQ Rub by Meat Church BBQ
- Yellow Mustard
- Dark Brown Sugar
- Honey
- Butter

Lay out the rack of ribs on a cutting board. Removing the membrane is optional. Coat both sides of the ribs in an even layer of the Kinder's Seasoning. Drizzle a thin line of mustard down the middle of the ribs (top side) and massage it around to get an even yellow layer. Then apply a coating of the Holy Gospel BBQ rub. Flip the ribs over and drizzle another line of mustard down the middle and spread it around as you did the top side. Add the layer of Holy Gospel BBQ rub. Now that the ribs are thoroughly seasoned, set them aside covered with foil as you prepare the grill.

Prepare your grill by cleaning the grate. Light the coals using a starter and close the top. Allow the temperature of the grill to reach ideally between 230-240 degrees. Once the proper temperature is reached, put the ribs on the grill, the meat side up, and close the lid. After three hours, check the ribs for even red coloring as this will indicate that the smoke is helping the bark develop by absorbing the smoke properly. Even distribution of a crusty exterior is key in this step. At this time, you can take the ribs out of the grill and lay them on a large sheet pan that is covered in a large piece of tin foil. Lay about 3 pads of butter across the top of the ribs. Take a handful of the brown sugar and sprinkle it evenly on the length of the ribs. Drizzle warm honey liberally to finish. Flip the ribs over and repeat this process. Leave the ribs' meat side down.

Wrap the ribs in the large sheet of foil like you're wrapping a gift. Put the wrapped ribs back on the grill, the meat side down, where they will spend the last two hours cooking. The honey, sugar, and butter glaze will carmalize and create its own sauce. After two hours, check the internal temperature of the ribs, which should read around 200 degrees. A temperature probe should be placed in the meat without touching the bone, as rib bones radiate more heat. Another way to check the doneness of ribs is to see how easily the bone pulls out. Barbecue masters know really well how ribs feel, but it takes a practiced hand to hone this skill.

Smoked Crab Legs

Smoking crab legs is a bit of a diversion from steaming them in a pot, but once I tried it, i didn't want to go back. Not only do they cook the meat so perfectly, but the shells also snap with little effort, making them much easier to eat. The crab meat slides out with ease, which seems to only happen if you're lucky with traditional steaming. Not to mention, smoked crab legs absolutely swim in butter and seasonings. If you've ever been to a crab restaurant where they serve crab legs in plastic bags of butter and seasonings, you will love this recipe. The crab legs cook relatively quickly, so it is feasible to make them last minute if you need to.

Ingredients:

- 5 lbs. of frozen snow crab legs
- ½ lb. of unsalted butter.
- 1 tablespoon of fresh parsley
- 1 Tablespoon of preferred barbecue rub
- ½ Teaspoon of Crab Boil seasoning or Old Bay
- Juice of 1 whole lemon

Prepare your charcoal smoker by cleaning the grates and setting up for indirect cooking (this configuration varies depending on the type of grill or smoker you are using). Bring the temperature of the grill to 250 degrees.

In a saucepan, melt the butter over low heat and stir in all the seasonings and the lemon juice. Transfer the melted butter mixture to a large baking dish or aluminum pan and dip each cluster in the butter to coat completely. Keep the remaining butter on-hand to baste the crab legs with.

Arrange all the crab leg clusters on the grates of the smoker and allow them to smoke for 30 minutes. Baste the crab legs with the butter mixture about halfway through cooking. After 30 minutes, remove the legs from the heat and transfer to a sheet pan. Baste with the remaining butter and serve immediately with extra lemon wedges and cocktail sauce.

Onion Jam

Cook time: 1 hour
Ingredients:

- 5 medium sized yellow onions
- 1 tablespoon of unsalted butter
- 2 tablespoons of white wine vinegar
- 2 tablespoons of grenadine
- 1 teaspoons of sugar
- 1 teaspoon of salt

Chop onions down into large chunks and add them to a food processor. Process onions until they are finely minced.

In a medium saucepan melt the butter and add the onions. While they are cooking, add the vinegar, grenadine, sugar, and salt. Continue to cook on medium high heat for an hour covered with a lid. The onions will caramelize and turn a deep golden brown when they are done. Store in airtight container in the refrigerator for up to a week.

Mac n' Cheese and Braised Short Rib Sandwich

This is a glorious mac and cheese recipe, and the best i have come across. One great use for it is to put it on a sandwich with the braised short rib (page 43) for an absolutely epic sandwich.

Ingredients:

- 1lb. of elbow macaroni (or cavatappi shells)
- 4 Tablespoons of butter
- 4 Tablespoons of flour
- 1 quart of whole milk
- 4 cups of shredded sharp cheddar cheese
- ½ cup of white cheddar cheese, grated
- Salt to taste
- Black Pepper
- ½ Teaspoon of paprika.

Cook pasta until al-dente, usually about 9 minutes in a large pot of boiling water. Drain and set to the side.

Using the same large pot (I don't like doing dishes), melt the butter over medium heat. Add the flour and constantly stir until you have a thick paste, known as a roux. Stir until the roux is smooth. Pour in milk and cook until the milk begins to thicken. Stir frequently with a whisk. Turn off the heat and add all the cheeses by the handfuls. Stir until the cheese sauce is smooth. Add macaroni and stir to coat.

Assemble the sandwich:
Spread mayonnaise on ciabatta rolls. Option to add steak sauce as well. Layer short rib meat and mac & cheese on the bun. Slice and enjoy your ugly-delicious sandwich with reckless abandon.

Breads and Baking

The Best and Most Versatile White Bread Recipe

I use this bread recipe for so many things because the results are so perfect each of the approximately 1,000 thousand times I've made it. This recipe can be used to shape into burger buns, rolls, and many more. It's that useful!

Makes two loaves of bread.
Ingredients:

- 6 1/2- 7 cups (780 grams) of bread flour
- 3 tablespoons of sugar
- 1 tablespoon of salt
- 2 tablespoons of shortening
- 2 packages (or 4 1/2 Teaspoons) of active dry yeast
- 2 ¼ cups of water warmed to 125 degrees
- 2 tablespoons of melted butter.

In a stand mixer fitted with a dough hook attachment, mix 3 ½ cups of flour, sugar, salt, shortening, and yeast. Add the warm water while the mixer is running on the 'stir' setting. Scrape down the bowl and increase the speed for 1 minute. Repeat this until the first portion of the flour is well incorporated (dough will look very sticky). Gradually add the remaining flour while the mixer is running and watch the dough form a smooth ball. The dough should feel light and tacky but workable. If the dough is firm, that would indicate that the bread will be denser.

Lightly flour a work surface and knead the dough for about 10 minutes by hand, adding very small amounts of flour if necessary.

Transfer the dough to a large, greased bowl and cover with plastic wrap. Let the dough proof for about 45 minutes or until it doubles in size.

Once the dough has doubled in size, punch it down and gently work it into a log. Grease two 9"x5" loaf pans. Cut the log in half with a knife and put each piece of dough into the two loaf pans. Spray a piece of plastic wrap with cooking spray and cover the loaves lightly with it. Allow the loaves to rise another 30-45 minutes or until they have doubled in size. Meanwhile, preheat your oven to 425 degrees. Bake the loaves for about 30 minutes or until golden brown.

When the loaves are finished baking, remove from the oven and flip them out of the pans onto a cooling rack. Allow them to cool completely. If you slice the bread too early, the crumb will have a gummy texture.

Tip: Shape into burger buns

Blueberry Cream Cheese Babka

Makes 2 loaves

For the cream cheese filling: blueberry preserves
- 3 cups of blueberries
- ¾ cups of sugar
- 1 tablespoon of lemon juice

Bring to a boil and reduce heat and simmer for 15 minutes until thickened. Let it cool in the fridge while the dough rises.

- 8 oz. of softened cream cheese.
- ½ cup of sugar

Whip together and set aside.

Babka dough
- 4 cups of all-purpose flour
- 1/3 cup of sugar + 1 tsp
- 1 tsp of kosher salt
- 2 ¼ tsp of active dry yeast
- 1 cup of warm milk (100-110 degrees)
- 2 eggs
- 1 tsp of vanilla
- 10 tbsp. of unsalted butter, softened and cut into cubes

In a large bowl, whisk together flour, sugar, salt, and set aside.
In a stand mixer, add the warm milk and sprinkle yeast on top. Add a teaspoon of sugar to help activate the yeast. Stir to combine and let it stand for 5 minutes until the yeast starts to foam. Add eggs, vanilla, and flour mixture to the yeast mixture. Mix on low to combine. Increase to medium speed and mix for minutes until the dough is smooth.
In a stand mixer, add the warm milk and sprinkle yeast on top. Add a teaspoon of sugar to help activate the yeast. Stir to combine and let it stand for 5 minutes until the yeast starts to foam. Add eggs, vanilla, and flour mixture to the yeast mixture. Mix on low to combine. Increase to medium speed and mix for minutes until the dough is smooth.

(Cont'd)

Add the cubes of softened butter one at a time while the dough is mixing. Mix until all the butter is incorporated and the dough becomes sticky.

Transfer to an oiled bowl covered with plastic and allow it to rise for 1 to 1 ½ hours until doubled in size. At this point, the dough can be refrigerated and baked the next day.

Once the dough has risen, knead lightly and divide in half. Roll each portion of dough in a 12" x 16" rectangle. Spread with half of the blueberry cream cheese mixture, leaving a ½" inch border on the edges. Starting on the long side, roll the triangle tightly to form a log. Repeat with the other rectangle of dough.

Starting an inch from the top of the log, make a slice down the length of the log, cutting all the way through to the end. Cut the second log the same way.

Line two 9"x5" in loaf pans with parchment paper and set aside.

Starting with the first log, twist the two sections over the top of each other and pinch to seal at the bottom. Repeat this step with the second log and place in loaf pans.
Cover each loaf lightly with plastic wrap and let it rise for 1 hour.

Bake at 350 degrees for 40 minutes or until a toothpick dipped in it comes out clean.

Optional: you can brush with a sugar syrup glaze to give the babka a shine. Heat 1 part sugar to 1 part water in a saucepan and cook over medium heat until the sugar dissolves, and brush the tops with a pastry brush.

Orange Blossom Cream Honey and Meyer Lemon Babka

For the crumble topping:
- 6 tablespoons of flour
- 8 tablespoons of white sugar
- 4 tablespoons of cold butter, cubed

For the filling:

- 8 oz. of cream cheese.
- ¼ cup of sugar.
- 2 tablespoons of orange blossom cream honey.
- 3 tablespoons of lemon juice.
- The zest of a Meyer lemon.
- A pinch of salt.

For this babka, use the same recipe to make the dough as with the blueberry cream cheese babka recipe.

How to form a babka wreath: once the loaf ends have been braided together, bring the top and bottom together to form a ring and pinch together. Bake at 350 degrees for 40 minutes or until a toothpick inserted in it comes out clean. Once the babka has cooled, sprinkle the crumble topping on top. Drizzle on more honey on top to finish.

One of my favorite things to do on the weekend is making Japanese Milk Bread or Shokupan. Shokupan is a sweet and incredibly soft white bread that utilizes the tangzhong method. To achieve the rectangular shape, it is sometimes made in a Pullman Pan, a sharp rectangular loaf pan with a lid that slides over top, which will help shape the loaf into a perfect rectangle. The Tangzhong method used in Japanese Milk Bread that gives it such pillowy softness consists of cooking a thick slurry of whole milk and flour that you will add to the dough later. This method is also very useful in making sweet, bread-like cinnamon rolls if you are looking to achieve ultimate softness. Note: If you don't have a Pullman Pan, you can use a loaf pan and seal it very tightly with foil so that the top of the bread will bake flatter.

Makes 2 loaves
For the Tangzhong:
- ½ cup of whole milk
- ½ cup of water
- ½ cup of bread flour

For the dough:
- 6 cups of bread flour (750 grams)
- 1/3 cup of dry non-fat milk powder (31 grams)
- 1/3 cup of sugar (70 grams)
- 2 teaspoons of kosher salt
- 2 ¼ teaspoons of Active Dry Yeast (1 package)
- 1 1/3 cups of whole milk warmed to 110 degrees
- 1 stick of unsalted butter, melted, plus an additional tablespoon for brushing.

Make the Tangzhong: In a saucepan over medium heat, combine the whole milk, water, and bread flour. Whisk constantly while cooking until the mixture converts to a thick pudding-like consistency. Take it off the heat and set aside.

In the bowl of a stand mixer fitted with a dough hook, whisk together flour, milk powder, sugar, salt, and yeast. Pour in the milk, tangzhong, and melted butter as it is stirring and mix until it forms a ball. Transfer to a lightly floured work surface and knead into a tight smooth ball. Put the dough in a greased bowl and cover it with plastic wrap. Allow it to rise in a warm place for about 1-1 ½ hours or until it doubles in size.

Preheat the oven to 375 degrees. Prepare two Pullman pans (or 2 regular 9" x 5" loaf pans) by spraying thoroughly with baking spray. Be sure to coat the underside of the door that slides over the top of the pan with non-stick spray as well and set aside.

When the dough has finished proofing, divide it in half and roll each half into oval-shaped logs. Transfer the dough logs to the pans and brush the tops with melted butter. Cover each loaf pan with its respective top by gently sliding it on. You may see the dough pushing out through tiny openings on the sides while it expands. This is okay and will not be a problem while it bakes.

After the loaves have finished the second rise, bake for about 35-40 minutes. Let them cool slightly before removing the lids. After carefully removing the lids, flip the loaves out onto a wire rack and allow them to cook completely. Slice the loaves into thick slices and enjoy within a few days or freeze.

Shokupan (Japanese Milk Bread)

The night I made bao the first time, I think my life was forever changed. I bought an instant mix and it turned out really well. It was a sensation and I reveled in the glory of praise from friends and family for achieving such culinary finery. A month later, I wanted to make it again just to show off. With nothing but confidence, I purchased the same mix and started making them later that night, but unbeknownst to me, it wasn't in the cards. They were a total disaster. They were incredibly hard and tough for reasons I couldn't understand. I rushed out to the store and bought another box of mix, determined to quickly reattempt it. No mistakes this time. The second batch was even worse. My guests were super nice about it, but I knew inside I would never recover. I vowed that I would not endure this embarrassment ever again. So for the last couple of years, I have made and perfected a bao recipe that has redeemed a very cringe-inducing memory that is sure to never reoccur (in the bao capacity). If you use this recipe, you will have an amazing result and you will be revered. The moral of this story is a cautionary tale of trusting box mixes implicitly and that sometimes massive failure in the kitchen could lead you to make something fantastic. What a metaphor for life!

Makes 12-18 buns.
- 2 teaspoons of active dry yeast
- ¾ cup of water heated to 110-120 degrees
- 3 tablespoons of sugar
- 2 ½ cups of bread flour (300 grams)
- 1 ½ tablespoons of dry milk powder
- 2 teaspoons of salt
- ½ teaspoon of baking soda
- 4 tablespoons (1.8 oz.) of solid pork fat

Mix the warm water, yeast, and sugar in a small bowl and let the yeast bloom for about 5 minutes.

Meanwhile, in a large bowl, thoroughly combine the bread flour, dry milk powder, salt, and baking soda. Using your hands, break up the pork fat and mix it into the flour mixture. The dough should be sandy and hold shape when you clump it in your hands. Now add the yeast and water and form a dough. Knead by hand until you have a smooth, elastic ball, which should take about 8-10 minutes.

Transfer the dough to an oiled bowl and cover with plastic wrap. Allow it to rise in a warm place for 45 minutes or until doubled in size.

Once the dough has risen, punch it down to form a ball again. Lay out a baking sheet lined with parchment to the side and have an extra-long piece of plastic wrap on top of it. On a lightly floured surface, pull off golf ball-sized pieces of dough and roll it into a ball. Put the ball on the parchment but underneath the plastic wrap. Continue this process until you have 12-18 uniform balls formed and placed under the plastic wrap. This is the best way to keep the dough from forming a skin and helps it rise properly. Allow the dough balls to rest for about 30 minutes.

After the second rise, lightly flour your work surface. Take one of the dough balls and roll it flat using a small rolling pin or a straight drinking glass. Roll over it only about 3 times, as it should look like an oval. Take the bottom of the oval and fold it "hamburger style" to meet the top. Set it back on the sheet pan under the plastic wrap. Repeat until you have rolled all the dough balls into little taco shapes.
Allow them to rise again for about 30 minutes.

Toward the end of the last dough rise, take a large piece of parchment paper and cut it into 12-18 1"x1" square sheets. The bao will set on top of these while steaming and prevent them from sticking to your steamer. Prepare a stove top steamer or bamboo steamer basket. Wrap the lid of your steamer (or the top of your bamboo steamer) in a large kitchen tea- towel (tying it at the top) and place it on top of the steamer basket. This will lessen condensation from settling on the bao while it steams.

With the steam going strong, place the bao on the parchment squares and into the steamer, spacing them out. Once you have fit as many as you can in one batch, close the steamer and do not disturb or open the lid for 10 minutes. After 10 minutes, open the top and remove it from the steam source. The buns should be big and fluffy. Remove the buns and let them cool on a cooling rack. Repeat this process for the remaining batches.

Serve them immediately with your favorite meats and fillings. Show these babies a good time.

Flour Tortillas

This is the recipe that made me want to compile recipes in a physical book. I spent months working on just tortillas. I'm obsessed with them, and I can talk about making them all day to anyone who will listen. My sister had to fight me for this recipe and I kind of ramble it off to her a little incorrectly on purpose just to mess with her. (I won't do that to you though, I promise) There are a vast array of different tortilla types and methods of making them that I love experimenting with. I chose a basic flour tortilla recipe to share here because it's the one I've spent the most time as a novice and can confirm that it works so very well every time. There is a popular restaurant not far from where I live called "Juan's Flaming Fajitas" and it's everything that the name promises. It has a very long wait list pretty much all the time. I think it deserves a Michelin star and I've celebrated my last two birthdays there. Anyway, there is a big window to the kitchen where you can watch someone make the insanely good tortillas in mass quantities. I can be found in front of this window, arms folded, watching for just long enough to be a weirdo. I try to play it off like I'm a bored patron waiting for my table to be ready, but I'm not, I'm at my highest entertainment level. Now that I've confessed what a creep I can be about tortillas in a published work and can die happy, Here is what I came up with:

Makes 24 tortillas
- 3 cups of all-purpose flour (360 grams)
- 2 Teaspoons of fine sea salt
- 2 teaspoons of baking powder
- ¼ cup (55 grams) of Manteca Pork Lard. This cannot be substituted, it is crucial.
- 1 ¼ cups of very hot water (may add a few tablespoons more if you live in a dry climate)

Whisk together the flour, salt, and baking powder in a large bowl. Add the pork fat to the bowl and break it up with your hands into pea-sized pieces. The dough should clump easily in your hand when the lard is combined well enough. Pour in the hot water and mix with your hands. After mixing for a minute or so, a dough should begin to form. Continue kneading for about 8 minutes until you have a smooth ball. Let the dough rest in the bowl covered with plastic wrap for about 30 minutes.

After the dough has rested, roll pieces into golf-ball sized balls. Let the balls rest covered on the counter with plastic wrap over them.

Preheat a cast-iron skillet or a komal on the stove to high heat. Using a rolling pin, lightly flour your surface and roll the balls into a flat disk. If you have a tortilla press you can use it here. If you are looking for a large, thin, amoeba-shaped tortilla, roll the dough out so that it is thin enough to see your work surface through it. Throw the tortilla onto the hot cooking surface and let it cook on one side until you can see it bubbling. Flip over and cook the other side for about 15 seconds until brown spots appear. Place the hot tortilla in a receptacle (this will allow the tortilla to steam and become soft and pliable) and repeat these steps as you work through the batch. Store in an airtight container for a few days at room temperature or longer if you keep them refrigerated.

New York Bagels

I have spent a lot of time in the kitchen researching the two classic New York staples: bagels and pizza dough. I have gone to silly lengths to try to recreate a perfect New York-style bagel in my kitchen, which is located, as you know by now, in the desert. I have set up a humidifier before and have used different types of bottled water. I was kind of hell-bent on proving that a true NY bagel can be duplicated, but I have since toned down on being such a nerd about this subject. I am here to tell you; you do not need to do any of these things to make a great, fantastic bagel at home, but I do concede that NYC does magical things to food that I can get really close to but maybe not exactly arrive, and that's okay.

Ingredients:
Makes 8 bagels

- 2 ½ teaspoons of active dry yeast
- 4 ½ teaspoons of granulated sugar
- 1 ¼ cups of water, warmed to 110 degrees
- 3 ½ cups of bread flour (440 grams)
- 1 ½ teaspoons of salt
- Everything Bagel seasonings, sesame seeds, or poppy seeds as topping
- Large pot of water

In a small bowl, dissolve the active dry yeast in ½ cup of the warm water with sugar. Let the yeast proof for about 5 minutes and then stir it.

Whisk together the flour and salt in a large bowl. In the center of the flour mixture, pour in the yeast and sugar. Pour the remaining water (1/3 cup) into the flour mixture. You may add a few extra tablespoons of water if needed. The dough should be somewhat firm to the touch.

Sprinkle flour on a work surface and knead the ball of dough by hand for about 10 minutes. If using a stand mixer with a dough hook attachment, let it run for about 5 minutes or until the dough is smooth. Use vegetable oil to grease a large bowl and place your dough in with plastic wrap covering the top. Let it rise in a draft-free place (I usually use my oven—turned to the bread-proof setting) for 1 hour or until doubled in size. Once the dough has doubled, knead it a couple of times and let the dough rest covered for about 10 minutes.

Using a food scale, divide the dough into 8 equal pieces. Gently roll the dough into a ball and push your thumb down into the center of the ball to form a hole. Roll the ring of dough around your thumb while pulling outward to gently stretch the dough and place on a parchment-lined baking sheet. Repeat with the rest of your dough balls. Cover the dough ring with plastic wrap and let them rest while you prepare the boiling water.

Preheat your oven to 425 degrees.

Fill a large pot about halfway with water and bring to a boil. Reduce the heat down if it is at a rolling boil. Carefully drop the dough rings (3 at a time) into the boiling pot of water (almost like you are frying donuts). When the bagels float to the top, flip them over and boil for about two minutes on each side.

Using a slotted spoon, remove bagels from the boiling water and place them on a parchment-lined baking sheet. Quickly sprinkle on desired toppings while the bagels are still wet.

Bake the bagels in the oven for 20-25 minutes or until they are golden brown. Allow it to cool completely on a wired rack before slicing.

Perfect Pizza Dough

Perfecting pizza dough is a constant pursuit in my life and there are a couple of things that I have found to be essential in my research: 00 (double zero) flour, and you must get a pizza stone. Yes, you can make a delicious and tasty pan pizza at home without these things or an expensive outdoor pizza oven. But to get that crispy yet stretchy Neapolitan crust, you need a couple of special items. If you have these things at your disposal, you'll be golden. If you can't find 00 flour in your grocery store, it is easily available on-line and it's great to have on hand for homemade pasta as well.

Makes 2 large balls of dough

- 1 teaspoon of fine sea salt
- ½ teaspoon of sugar
- 2 ½ cups of water warmed to 100 degrees
- 1 package of active dry yeast (7 grams)
- 1 kg (2.2 lbs.) of 00 flour
- Extra Virgin Olive Oil

In a measuring cup, measure out the warm water and add salt, sugar, and yeast. Let the yeast bloom for about five minutes.

In a separate mixing bowl, measure out the flour and whisk around to break up any lumps. Make a well in the center of the flour and pour in the yeast and water mixture. Mix the flour and water until a dough starts to form.

Scoop out the dough onto a lightly floured surface and knead by hand for about 5-7 minutes. A smooth and elastic ball of dough will begin to form. Drizzle a small amount of extra virgin olive oil on the dough while kneading to smooth it out. Drizzle olive oil into the large mixing bowl and place the dough in it, turning it over to coat in the oil. Cover with plastic wrap and allow it to rise in a warm place until it doubles in size for about 30 minutes.

After the dough has risen, cut it into two separate 16 oz. Dough balls and let them rest covered for another 30 minutes.

Let the dough rise in the fridge overnight, or up to 2 days, covered in plastic wrap. This is referred to as a 'cold rise' and it helps the dough to develop more stretch and a more pronounced flavor with fermentation. However, you can certainly use the dough right away if you need to. The following day, take the dough out of the fridge and allow it to come to room temperature before rolling it out to make pizza.

Save Room For Dessert

Arroz Con Leche

I was lucky enough to take a trip to the Dominican Republic for my bestie Allex's wedding. It was gorgeous and dreamy, and I think about it often.
We took a long ride through the countryside of the island and toured a plantation that produced cacao, vanilla, coffee, and many other exports. They showed us step by step how the cocoa beans are harvested and the process behind making very fine chocolate. Inside of a small, pink, one-room house, there was a small oven and a bed. There was an incredibly delicious aroma coming from this tiny house, which was a mix between warm sugar and caramel but even better. Inside the kitchen, a woman was stirring a huge stockpot full of Arroz Con Leche, or 'rice with milk,' which is a Spanish rice pudding made with milk, sugar, and cinnamon. She gave us a sample of it, and it was so good I could've eaten the whole stockpot of it. This dessert is so simple and delicious and one of my favorite desserts in the whole world.
Cook time: 1 hour. Serves: 2-4

Ingredients:

- 1 cup of long-grain white rice
- 2 cinnamon sticks
- 1 teaspoon of pure vanilla extract
- ¼ teaspoons of salt
- 2 ½ cups of water
- 4 cups of whole milk
- 1 cup of white sugar
- Top with cinnamon, rum raisins, your favorite fruit, shredded coconut, or dates.

In a large pot, combine the white rice, cinnamon sticks, salt, vanilla, and water. Bring to a boil and let it boil for about 2 minutes. Reduce the heat to low, cover the pot, and simmer for about 15 minutes, stirring often to prevent the rice from sticking to the bottom. Add the milk and continue to let it simmer for another 15 minutes. Pour in the sugar and stir to combine. Let the rice continue to simmer for another interval of 15 minutes. At this point, the rice should reach a thick pudding-like consistency. If not, turn the heat higher and bring it back to a boil about 2 minutes. Take it off the heat and allow it to cool. Serve with your favorite toppings.

Baked pears are one of the easiest and most delicious warm desserts. I love to make these in the Fall or around Thanksgiving because the flavors are warm, but it's on the lighter side after a heavy meal. Bosc pears are a particularly luscious variety. So when they bake, the released juices mix with the topping and make a sweet fruit gel. The salted whip on the side gives a nice balance to the sweetness.

Serves 4
Ingredients:

- 4 Large Bosc pears, cut in half.
- 4 Tablespoons of Pure Maple Syrup
- 1 Teaspoon of cinnamon
- ¼ Cup of brown sugar
- A few drops of apple cider vinegar

Salted Honey Whip

- 1 cup of heavy cream
- ¼ confectioners' sugar
- ¼ tsp of fine sea salt
- 3 second pour of desert honey

Combine all ingredients in a large mixing bowl. With a stand mixer with a whisk attachment or a hand mixer. Beat heavy cream mixture until stiff peaks. Dollop on top of milkshakes, coffees or desserts.

Slice 4 Bosc pears in half, keeping the stems intact. Scoop out the seeds and set aside.

With the cut side up, drizzle maple syrup, cinnamon, brown sugar, and a few drops of apple cider vinegar. Bake at 350 degrees for 30 minutes or until the tops are brown and bubbling.

Baked Bosc Pear with Salted Honey Whip

Amy's Meyer Lemon Cookies

Delightful lemony cookies that melt in your mouth.

Amy's Meyer Lemon Cookies
- 1 cup of unsalted butter, softened
- ¾ cup of granulated sugar
- 1 egg
- The zest of one Meyer lemon
- 2 cups of all-purpose flour
- ½ teaspoon of baking powder
- ½ teaspoon of salt

For the glaze:
- 1 ½ cups of powdered sugar
- 2 tablespoons of lemon juice
- 1 tablespoon of heavy cream
- 1/8 teaspoon of salt

Preheat the oven to 375 degrees. In a stand mixer with a paddle attached, cream together butter and sugar until light and fluffy. Add the egg and mix until well combined. Add lemon zest and slow the mixer to stir.

In a separate bowl, whisk together flour, baking powder, and salt. Add the dry mix gradually to the butter mixture until well combined.

Line a baking sheet with parchment paper. Scoop tablespoon-sized balls of cookie dough, roll them into balls and place them on the baking sheet. Press down on them slightly to flatten them.

Bake the cookies for 8 minutes, but no more than 9 minutes. The cookies should be done in the middle but not browned so that they stay light. Transfer to a cooling rack. Whisk together the ingredients for the glaze and dip each cookie right-side-up into the glaze. Scrape off excess. Sprinkle a small amount of lemon zest on top for garnish. Return them to the baking sheet for the icing to set.

Ganny's Pound Cake

My Great-Grandmother's rich and irresistible pound cake that we force my Aunt to make every time we visit.

Makes 2 cakes
Ingredients:

- 1 pound (2 sticks of butter or margarine)
- 1 tablespoon of shortening
- 3 cups of granulated sugar (600 grams)
- 3 cups of all-purpose flour (380 grams)
- 6 eggs
- 1 8 oz. package of sour cream
- ¼ teaspoon of baking soda (added with sour cream)
- 1 teaspoon of almond or vanilla extract

Preheat the oven to 325 degrees. In a stand mixer with the paddle attachment, beat together butter and shortening. Add sugar, one cup at a time. Add eggs, one at a time. Add flour and sour cream and vanilla extract. Let the mixer run for a few minutes to fully incorporate.

Thoroughly butter and flour a large bundt pan. Pour the cake batter into the bundt pan and bake for about 1 ½ hours or until a toothpick comes out clean. Serve with whipped cream and berries or all by itself.

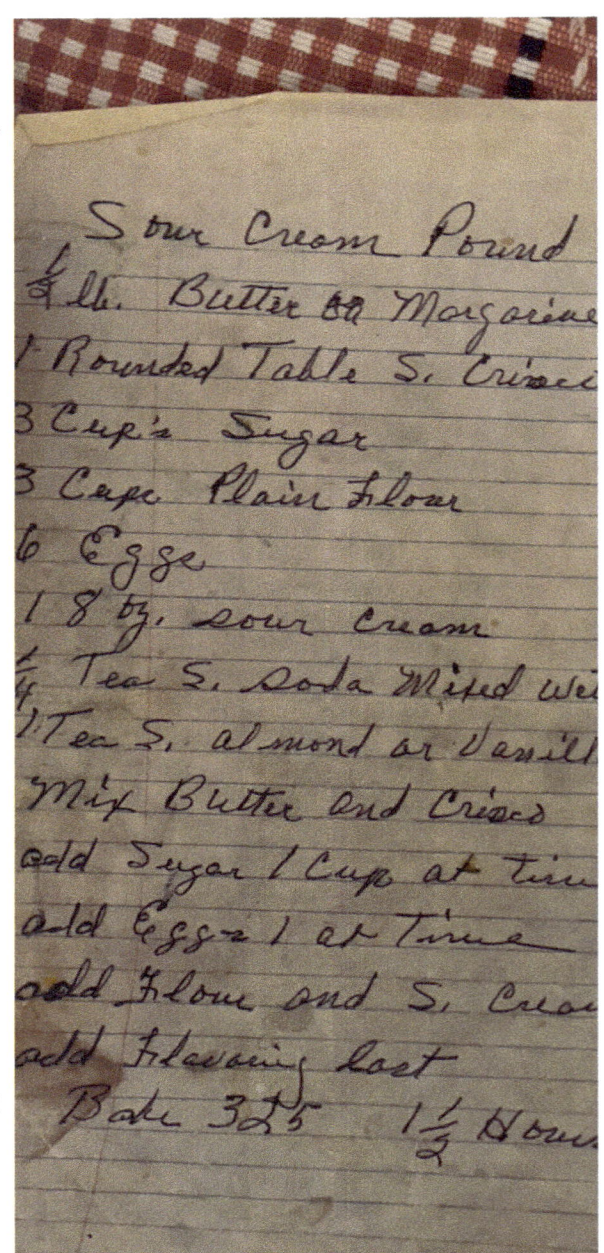

Desert Honey

Honey Toast

I think my bestie Allex and I were 19 or 20 when she took me to Shuseki, a popular Japanese Restaurant that was here in our Korea Town in Las Vegas. This restaurant was a deep dive into authentic Japanese cuisine and had a full array of ramen, udon, soba, as well as many other items. It was here that I first laid eyes (and my taste buds) on Honey Toast. Honey Toast is a is a beautiful buttery box of warm toast filled with ice cream, fruit or other assorted toppings. It is a desert staple in many Japanese restaurants and a must try not only because it's such a treat but because everyone's head will turn when they see it coming to your table. My version has some of my favorite ice cream toppings but of course there's a million different things you could put on yours to make it your own masterpiece.

Ingredients:

- 1 loaf of Shokupan, sliced in half (page 91)
- 1 tablespoon of unsalted butter
- Vanilla Bean ice cream-store-bought
- Green Tea ice cream
- Ube Ice Cream (purple yam)
- Orange Blossom Honey
- Whipped Cream (for topping)
- Strawberries, kiwi, dragon fruit, and banana slices (for topping)

Slice your loaf of Shokupan in half so that you have two separate "boxes". Store one of them for later. With cut side up, hallow out most of the bread inside but leave enough so that the sides are sturdy. Brush softened butter on the outside of the box and heat up a small frying pan. Toast all sides of the bread box and set it cut-side up on a serving platter. Fill the inside with scoops of ice cream and sliced fruit, building up to the top. Top with whipped cream, fruit and drizzle with honey. Serve immediately.

Leche Quemada Ice Cream with Vanilla Bean

This idea came from my mom, who gave me a recipe for Leche Quemada candy that belonged to a friend she had while living in Houston, Texas. When I tried it, the candy didn't turn out quite right, but I couldn't get over the idea of making it into an ice cream flavor somehow. Leche Quemada (also known as Mexican Burnt Milk Candy) is a chewy, warm caramel made with brown sugar. It is a popular treat in Mexico that is a part of the sweet childhood memories of many people. When I made this on my blog, I got a message that was so gratifying; it is the reason that I kept going and brought this book to you. To paraphrase, it read: "I live in Oaxaca. All my life that I have lived here, I did not know how the (Leche Quemada) was prepared and you taught us how we can do it. I will try your recipe." I love the fact that, in this age, we can reach and connect with people through food all over the world who we would never have had the opportunity to connect with before. There has been no better time to create.

In this recipe, I make the candy itself and thin it out to make a ribbon that swirls in the vanilla ice cream. It is quite dreamy and not very difficult to make. Enjoy!

Yield: 2 Pints. Preparation time: 4 hours

For the Vanilla custard base:
- 2 cups of whole milk
- 2 cups of heavy whipping cream
- 1 vanilla bean pod (or 2 teaspoons of pure vanilla extract)
- 4 egg yolks
- ½ cup of sugar

For the Leche Quemada:
- 1 (14 oz.) can of evaporated milk
- 1 cup of packed dark brown sugar
- 1 teaspoon of ground cinnamon
- A pinch of kosher salt
- 4 oz. of marshmallow cream
- A handful of chopped pecans
- 1 tablespoon of butter

(Cont'd)

In a medium-sized saucepan, bring the milk and heavy cream to a boil. Split the vanilla bean pod down the center and scrape out the seeds. Once the cream mixture begins to thicken, add the vanilla seeds and turn off the heat. Put the whole vanilla bean pod in the saucepan and cover with a lid while you continue to the next step.

In a smaller saucepan, over medium-low heat, whip the egg yolks and the sugar together. Whip vigorously until it becomes pale and fluffy. Temper the eggs (gently raise the temperature) by adding a slow stream of the hot cream mixture. Slowly incorporate the rest of the cream. Once the egg and milk mixture is combined, continue to heat over low heat. When it is thick (about 180 degrees), remove the saucepan from the heat and allow it to cool. Transfer it to a bowl, cover with plastic wrap, and allow it to chill for at least 4-6 hours.

After the starter has sufficiently chilled, make the candy mix-in. In a saucepan, combine evaporated milk, brown sugar, cinnamon, and kosher salt. Stir this over medium-high heat until it starts to thicken but does not reach the softball stage (less than 200 degrees). Increase the heat and let it come to a rolling boil. As soon as it begins to boil, add the marshmallow cream and stir to combine. Turn the heat down to low and grab a small mixing bowl. Add a few scoops of the candy mixture to the mixing bowl and drop the pad of butter and a couple of tablespoons of cream in the middle. Let it sit and melt for a few seconds, then stir. It should look glossy and have a honey consistency. Add the chopped pecans in.

In the main saucepan with the rest of the candy, add a pad of butter, let it melt, and whip it in. Transfer it to a loaf pan and allow it to harden to candy. Set this aside to chop later.

Add the vanilla starter to your ice cream maker and allow it to churn for about 10 minutes. Drizzle a slow but steady stream of the Leche Quemada sauce while it is turning. Allow it to churn for another 5 minutes. Transfer to an airtight container and freeze until firm for about 6-8 hours. When it is ready to scoop, sprinkle with pieces of chopped candy and walnuts.

Desert Honey

Miss Moffet's Brownies

Miss Moffet's brownies are famous in our family and are so good that they caused a bit of controversy. Miss Moffet was a friend of my Great Grandmother and attended the Highland church with her in High Point, North Carolina around the 1950s. Miss Moffet was a beloved member of the church and was known for making absolutely delicious brownies. She was often begged to share this recipe by her fellow churchgoers, even to the point where the Priest was sent to her house to ask if she would be willing to share it to appease those who were upset. When you make it, you'll understand why. Little did they know, it's been on the back of the Hershey's Syrup can for decades but nevertheless, she declined to divulge it. But she loved my Great Grandma so much she only trusted her with it. These brownies have a textured richness that borders between a cake and a brownie, and the "boiled icing" is a deeply delicious chocolate glaze that is poured over the hot brownie and sinks into the cake.

Makes 9 Brownies sliced into Squares
Ingredients:
- 1 cup of All-purpose Flour
- 1 Stick of Unsalted Butter, softened
- 1 Cup of sugar
- 16 oz. of Hershey's Chocolate Syrup
- 4 eggs, beaten.
- 1 Tsp of Vanilla Extract
- A Pinch of salt

Boiled icing
- 1/3 Cup of Evaporated Milk
- 1 cup of sugar
- 1 stick of unsalted Butter
- ½ cup of semi-sweet chocolate chips

Preheat the oven to 350 degrees.

Grease a 9" inch square (22cm) cake pan and set aside.

In a large mixing bowl, combine all the brownie ingredients. Using a hand mixer or a stand mixer, mix on medium-high heat until combined and the butter is thoroughly incorporated. You may see small pieces of butter in the batter, but that's fine. Pour the batter into the greased cake pan and bake for about 40-50 minutes until the top of the cake springs back when touched. In the last 5 minutes or so of baking, prepare the icing.

In a medium saucepan, pour in the evaporated milk, sugar, and add the stick of butter.

While stirring, bring ingredients to a rolling boil. Allow it to boil for 60 seconds and remove the saucepan from the heat. While stirring constantly, add the ½ cup of chocolate chips until they are melted and well incorporated. The icing should have a glossy glaze consistency. Pour the hot icing over the hot cake and allow it to cool before serving. These are best served warm, and they last for about 5 days if covered and stored in the fridge.

Lemon Turmeric Tart

A lot of my friends and loved ones have food intolerances, and finding good dessert recipes that everyone can have can be a challenge. This Lemon Turmeric Tart is just as delicious, if not better than, a traditional lemon custard and the crust is a toasty and crunchy complement to the smooth tart filling. Turmeric not only gives it a vibrant yellow hue, but turmeric is known to be helpful with inflammation. I use gluten-free graham crackers made by a brand called Pamela's because they are thicker and more flavorful than regular brands. Therefore, I recommend giving them a try. It's also easy to make! What's not to love?!

Yield: 8 slices
For the crust:
- 6 gluten-free graham crackers (5 oz.)
- 1 cup of toasted oat flour
- ¼ cup of coconut oil
- ¼ cup of high-quality maple syrup

For the lemon filling:
- 1/3 cup (75 ml) of freshly squeezed lemon juice, about 2 lemons
- 2 tablespoons of corn starch
- 1 cup of full-fat coconut milk
- 1/3 cup of maple syrup
- 2 tablespoons of organic coconut oil
- Teaspoon of ground turmeric
- Zest of 1 lemon
- Lemon slices for garnish

Preheat the oven to 350 degrees. Spray a 10" inch round tart pan with baking spray and set aside.

In a food processor, add graham crackers and oat flour and pulse until you have fine crumbs. Add the coconut oil and maple syrup and pulse a few times until the crust becomes dough-like. Spoon the dough into the tart pan and press it flat while molding it to the edges. You can use the bottom of a glass to help spread out the uneven parts. Bake the crust for about 20 minutes until it is toasted and golden brown and let it cool while you make the filling.

Make the lemon filling: In a small saucepan, whisk the lemon juice and corn starch to break up the lumps. Add the coconut milk, maple syrup, coconut oil, turmeric, and vanilla extract and whisk to combine. Turn the heat to medium and bring it to a simmer, whisking until it begins to thicken to almost a pudding consistency for about 7-8 minutes. Once it has thickened, take it off the heat and let it cool. While it is cooling, it will continue to thicken a bit more.

Once the filling has cooled, pour it onto the tart crust and smooth it out, leaving about a 1/8-inch border around the edges. Put the tart in the refrigerator to cool for about 4 hours.

Once the tart is cool, decorate with lemon slices and zest. Push the removable bottom of the tart pan up to remove the ring. Use the bottom to support transferring the tart to a cake plate or serving platter and slide it off. Slice and serve.

Mochi Donuts

If you've never had the pleasure of trying mochi donuts, I absolutely insist that you search for a place that makes them near you and run—don't walk—to get them. Stop here and avoid all this trouble. If not, then you've come to the right page and the trouble will be worth it! Mochi Donuts were made famous by a bakery in Japan called "Mr. Donut." They are, understandably so, a sensation and have become very popular in the U.S. in the last couple of years.

You can make something very close to the store-bought legends at home. The texture is light, airy, and chewy all at the same time. It's mesmerizing and I'm so glad that they are a thing! But I must caution you: this is technically the biggest baking challenge in this book (second only to bao). However, if you made my yeast donut recipe, then this won't be that much more difficult, and you'll enjoy it all the same. The trick is getting the texture of the dough right; it will be a very soft dough that comes together just enough to be workable. It is very sticky, contrasting with the dough of the yeast donuts and bread, whereas those are a bit denser and more forgiving. The original mochi donuts are made into a ring of 8 individual balls and fried, but my home version opts for shaping them into a ring of 5 larger balls (purely out of laziness). But you are welcome to make them look more like the real thing. I tried a couple of different recipes that I found on-line and combined the best of those worlds to create a recipe that uses the least amount of specialty ingredients and is easiest to follow. This is a fun weekend project and you might as well get some practice under your belt because your loved ones will request them again! Let's dive in.

Yield: 8 donuts depending on the size and shape you want.   Cook time: approximately 2 hours.

For the dough (in order of appearance):
- 6 tablespoons of unsalted butter, melted
- 2 large eggs, beaten
- 1 cup (237 milliliters) of whole milk heated to 100-110 degrees
- 1 ½ teaspoons of active dry yeast
- ¼ cup of sugar
- 2 ½ cups of tapioca flour (300 grams)
- 1 teaspoon of pure vanilla extract
- 1 ¼ cup of all-purpose flour (151 grams)
- ½ teaspoon of fine salt
- 1 quart of safflower oil for frying

For the glaze:
- 2 cups of powdered sugar
- 3-4 tablespoons of whole milk
- ¼ teaspoon of coconut extract

(Cont'd)

Melt the butter and set it aside to let it cool. Whisk two eggs in a small bowl and set aside. In the bowl of a stand mixer fitted with a paddle attachment, add the warm milk, yeast, and ½ teaspoon of sugar. Allow the yeast to bloom for about 5 minutes.

In a separate mixing bowl, place a fine-mesh sieve (strainer) over the top of it. Add both flours and pass them through the sieve, discarding lumps or hard pieces left behind.

Once the yeast has bloomed in the stand mixer, add all the sugar, beaten eggs, melted butter, and vanilla. Turn the mixer on low speed and let it mix the dough until it's combined. Add the flour mixture and salt one cup at a time to the mixer, letting the last cup to fully incorporate before adding the next one. At this point, the dough will be very soft, like a thick batter. Increase the speed of the mixer and beat on medium-high for 3-5 minutes. The dough will develop gluten as it is being kneaded at a higher speed at this stage. Thus, it is best to resist the urge to add more flour. While the mixer is going, prepare a large mixing bowl by greasing it with vegetable oil and set it aside. After about 5 minutes of beating at high speed, scoop out the dough onto a very lightly floured surface and dust your hands with some flour. Knead the dough with your hands, intermittently flouring just your hands in the process to be able to work with it. Scoop up the dough with a bench scraper (or a spatula if you don't have one) and transfer it to a large mixing bowl that you have prepped. Cover the dough with plastic wrap and allow it to rise in a warm place for 1 hour but no more than 1 hour and 20 minutes.

While the dough is rising, there are a few things you can prepare:

- Pour the frying oil in a large Dutch oven or a heavy-bottomed pot. Affix a candy thermometer to the side. Heat the oil to 325 but no more than 350 degrees.

- Make the glaze. Whisk together all the glaze ingredients. You can add a different flavoring if you choose.

- Line a baking sheet with parchment paper and place a cooling rack over it.

- Cut out 8-10 4"x 4" inch square papers out of the parchment paper, one for each donut ring, and set aside.

Once the dough has risen, scrape it onto a lightly floured work surface. Knead it a few times and cover most of it with plastic wrap (you will pull the pieces of dough out as you knead them). Pull out 5 pieces of dough and roll them into balls. For consistency and best results, use a food scale to determine the weight of each, which may be around 10 grams per ball depending on how large you would like your donuts to be. Put each set of 5 dough balls on the parchment squares in a concentric circle and set aside. Continue until you have used all the dough to form rings. Brush each ring with a small amount of water, which will help them stick together once they are in the frying oil.

Using a skimmer or a spatula, slide the donut (still on the parchment) into the frying oil. Fry no more than 2 at a time so that the temperature of the oil doesn't drop. Fry 1 minute per side, or until you see it float to the top and turn golden brown underneath. Flip it and let the other side fry for 1 minute as well. Take out the donuts with the skimmer and place them on the sheet pan with the cooling rack. While the donut is still hot, dip it in the glaze and set it back on the rack. At this point, you can cover with additional toppings if desired.

Let the donuts cool and enjoy! They can last for up to 2 days if refrigerated.

Melt In your Mouth Cookies

My Aunt found this recipe from my great-grandmother socked away in a jewelry box and I am so glad she did! This cookie recipe utilizes an interesting baking technique that incorporates hard-boiled egg yolks into the cookie dough. This method produces a very tender and buttery crumb (that melts in your mouth) because the egg yolks bind with gluten and create a light texture. However, the proportions of this recipe may shock you. It calls for an entire pound of margarine, but a truckload of margarine or butter is very common in old-fashioned southern recipes and that's why it's so good. Try it at least once to experience a cookie that truly melts in your mouth.

Makes 2 dozen cookies

Ingredients:
- 1 cup of granulated sugar
- 1 pound of margarine or butter
- 5 hard-boiled egg yolks
- 5 cups of all-purpose flour
- 2 teaspoons of vanilla
- A pinch of salt

Preheat the oven to 350 degrees. Beat sugar and margarine in a stand mixer until light and fluffy. Add hard-boiled egg yolks, flour, vanilla, and salt. Form the dough into balls and place on a cookie sheet lined with parchment. Bake for about 10 minutes, or until set and barely browned on the bottom. The trick is to not overcook the cookies.
Transfer to a cooling rack and allow it to cool.

Sweet Mojito Mint Ice Cream

If you live in an extreme climate like I do, you may have found that maintaining a healthy herb garden can be a bit difficult. Herbs don't do well in the desert heat except for the early spring months so it is best to try to do your best gardening at this time of year. One herb that does very well in a dry climate Mojito mint, which is a very mild and sweet mint variety ideally used in a mojito making. It has large leaves and can grow very wildly with little effort. My mojito mint plant absolutely took over this year and I had to find a good way to use a lot of it at once, and thus this ice cream recipe was born. This recipe certainly can be made with another variety of mint that is more accessible to you, I would just suggest using a bit less to achieve that sweet mild mint taste.

Yields 4 pints   Prep time : 10 minutes
Chill time: 8 hours

- 1.6 oz. of mojito mint leaves
- 4 cups of heavy cream
- 2 cups of whole milk
- 5 oz. of powdered sugar
- 2 tablespoons of pure vanilla extract
- ¼ cup of fresh lime juice
- The zest of two limes
- A pinch of kosher salt
- Organic green food coloring (optional)
- 12" inch square piece of cheese cloth and string for tying it
- Ice cream maker

Using a large molcajete or mortar and pestle, muddle the mojito mint leaves into a fine paste. Lay down the square piece of cheese cloth and put the muddled mint leaves in the middle of the cloth. Tie the corners together with string or twine so that you have a secure sachet or pouch.

In a large bowl, stir together the cream, milk, powdered sugar and vanilla extract, lime juice, lime zest, pinch of kosher salt, and the optional food coloring. Take the mint sachet and squeeze out some of the oil into the cream mixture and drop it in. From here, you can let the mint cold-steep in the cream over night to develop the flavor or at least four hours. If you are making this the same day, periodically pull out the mint sachet and express the oil out to infuse more flavor. Once the starter has spent sufficient time steeping, pour it into your ice cream maker and church until it is smooth and creamy. Store in an airtight container in the freezer and allow it to freeze for at least 3 hours before serving. Scoop into a glass bowl rimmed with salt and garnish with mint leaves.

The Sub Shop Cookie

I am a firm believer that some of the best chocolate chip cookies in the world are born in sandwich places or "sub shops". Port of Subs, Jimmy John's, all those places seem to have the strongest cookie game and I set out to crack the code. I think this recipe, with the secret ingredient of vanilla pudding mix, just about cracks the code. You get the chewy, caramelized cookie we all love so much with a very smooth vanilla flavor, not achieved by actual vanilla extract. A little sprinkle of flaky salt over those huge chocolate chunks never made anyone mad, ever. Without further ado, here is my long-perfected and slaved-over chocolate chip cookie recipe.

Makes 8 very large cookies

Preheat Oven to 300 Degrees

- 1 ½ Sticks of butter
- ½ Cup Packed Dark Brown Sugar
- ½ Cup of White Sugar
- 3 oz. of Instant Vanilla Pudding Mix
- 2 large eggs

Beat together the first 5 ingredients until fluffy

In a separate bowl, whisk together:

- 2 ½ cups of bread flour or All-Purpose Flour
- 1 teaspoon of baking soda
- 1 teaspoon of baking powder
- 1 Bag of Ghirardelli Chocolate Chips

Shape the dough into large balls. Arrange on a cookie sheet and bake for about 15-20 minutes or until golden brown on the edges.
Sprinkle a tiny pinch of sea salt on top of each cookie while they are still hot out of the oven.

Desert Honey

Butter Coconut Cream Cakes

I am low-brow at heart and can't deny that this spongy gift to the world isn't one of my favorite things. I put a little twist on this classic and made an easy little recipe. You don't even have to make those tedious foil molds! By all means, you can, but I was really frustrated real fast when I tried it. Make these for your friends and they'll think it's adorable that you: 1. Went to these lengths to duplicate this snack cake 2. Your inner child is alive and well.

Ingredients:

- 1 Box of Duncan Hines White Cake Mix
- ½ Cup of water
- 3 large egg whites (reserve yolks for pasta sauce ;)
- 1/3 cup of vegetable oil
- ¼ Cup of lime juice (cuts the "box mix cake" flavor that's distinct)

Preheat the oven to 350 degrees. Mix all the ingredients together. Spray and lay a parchment in a 9x9 square cake pan. Fill with batter and bake for 35 minutes or until an inserted knife is clean. Allow the cake to cook completely. Once cooled, cut into rectangles.

Fluffy filling:
Whip on high speed or with a whisk:
- 6 tablespoons of softened butter
- 1 jar of marshmallow fluff
- 1 cup of powdered sugar
- 3-4 drops of coconut extract
- 2 tablespoons of heavy cream
-

Fill a piping bag fitted with a star tip with marshmallow filling. Insert directly into the cake and fill. Repeat in a line down the center of each rectangle and serve.

Vanilla Bean Pan Dulce

Makes 4 cakes

For the icing:
- ½ cup of all-purpose flour
- 3 tablespoons of sugar
- 3 tablespoons of shortening
- 1 vanilla bean pod

For the cake:
- 1 ¼ cups of bread flour
- 1 egg
- 3 tablespoons of unsalted butter
- 1 teaspoon of active dry yeast
- 3 tablespoons of sugar
- ¼ cup of water
- Salt

Make the icing sheets by combining flour and shortening. Split the vanilla bean pod in half and using a paring knife, carefully scrape out the seeds and mix them with the flour and shortening. Roll the icing dough into 4 individual balls. Line a tortilla press with plastic wrap and press each ball into a flat disk and lay them to the side while you make the cakes.

Combine flour, egg, butter, yeast, sugar, water, and salt in a large bowl and knead with your hands until you have a smooth elastic dough. The dough will be on the sticky side, but you can add a tablespoon of flour to make it more workable. Cover the bowl with plastic wrap and allow it to rise in a warm place until it doubles in size.

After the dough finishes rising, cut it into 4 equal pieces and roll into balls. Prepare a sheet pan lined with a sheet of parchment paper. Lay the dough balls on the sheet pan, spacing about 3" apart. Lay a vanilla bean icing sheet on each of the four dough balls. Using a very sharp knife, carefully draw thin diagonal lines in the icing for the design. Allow them to rise again until doubled in size. Preheat the oven to 350 degrees.

Once the dough has finished its second rise, bake them for about 15 minutes or until they begin to turn golden brown. Place them on a rack cool before serving.

Beauty Bowl

I love Acai bowls and there was a time where I had to have one every other day after my workout. I made this "beauty bowl" at home because I decided to try making it with some super foods with real health benefits and also because it's pretty. In the photograph, I used a very fancy garnish called an apple swan. I learned how to cut the apple swan from watching the tutorial video produced by one of my favorite chefs of all time, the great Jaques Pépin. I recommend looking up the video and giving it a try. It is actually easy to do and so impressive as a garnish.

Serves 1

Beauty Bowl
- 1 cup of Skyr or Greek Yogurt
- ¼ teaspoon of Blue Spirulina
- Cacao nibs
- Blueberries
- Pineapple slices
- Raw Unfiltered Desert Honey
- Apple Swan Garnish (tutorial available on YouTube by Jaques Pépin)

Mix the yogurt base with the blue spirulina powder. The spirulina will produce a very vivid, natural hue. Top with the desired amount of listed toppings and drizzle with honey.

I've made donuts a lot over the years for my son and his friends, so this is my go-to super fluffy yeast donut recipe.

Yield: 12 donuts
Ingredients:

- 2 quarts of vegetable oil (for frying)
- 1 cup of whole milk (warmed to 90-100 degrees)
- 2 1/2 teaspoons (one package) of active dry yeast
- 2 eggs
- (1 stick/ 8TBSP)of butter, melted and cooled
- ¼ cup of granulated sugar
- 1 teaspoon of salt
- 4 cups of all-purpose flour, plus more for rolling out the dough

Pour the warm milk and yeast into a large bowl or the bowl of a stand mixer (with dough hook attachment).
Let it bloom for about 5 minutes. Add melted butter, eggs, sugar, and salt and mix to combine. Gradually add flour by the cupfuls. Sprinkle in a tablespoon of flour at a time if the dough is too sticky to handle. It should pull away from the sides, but you definitely don't want to add too much or they will be dense.
Coat a large mixing bowl with oil. Place the dough in a bowl to rise in a warm place for about an hour. It should double in size.
Divide the dough into 12 equal-sized pieces and roll into balls. Stick your finger down the center of the ball and twirl around to make a hole. If desired, you can use a very small circular biscuit cutter or narrow glass to cut a hole and have donut holes.
Place the shaped donuts on a parchment-covered baking sheet and cover with plastic wrap while you heat the oil.
Using a large pot or Dutch oven, affix a candy thermometer. Heat vegetable oil until it reaches 350 degrees.
Use a large spatula to handle the shaped donut and carefully lower it into the frying oil. The temperature of the oil will drop a bit, but just watch it to make sure it rebounds.
When the donut begins to brown, flip on the other side and let it fry for about 2 minutes per side. Repeat on the other side. Use a meat thermometer to check the internal temperature of the dough. It should be at least 150 degrees on the inside before you pull it. Remove the donut from the oil and place on a cooling wrap with a paper towel under it to drain.

Cold Drinks

Desert Honey

Coachella Valley Date Shake

A date shake is a popular treat where dates grow abundantly: the blistering hot desert of Coachella Valley and Palm Springs. I made a version that is "lower" in sugar and dairy-free. It's not quite as thick as the ones you may find at pit stops between Vegas and the middle of nowhere, but it is delicious.

Serves 1
Ingredients:

- Hot water (enough to submerge dates in)
- 5 or 6 large dates (pitted or non-pitted)
- Pinch of kosher salt
- 1 Tablespoon of Golden Monk fruit (a sugar-free brown sugar product, which is optional if you'd rather use the real stuff).
- 1 teaspoon of Saigon Cinnamon
- 1 Cup of oat milk (Or non-dairy milk of choice; I just wouldn't use coconut milk)
- 1 Tablespoon of prepared espresso (optional)
- Oat milk Vanilla ice cream
- Handful of ice

Method: Place the dates in a heat-proof bowl. Pour very hot water over the dates until they are covered. Add the next three ingredients, plus a dash of the cup of oat milk and let steep for 10 minutes.

Remove the dates and place them on a paper towel. Pinch the middle of the date and the large pit should come out easily. If you're using non-pitted, there's no need for this step.

Put the dates back into the steeping liquid. Pour the dates and liquid into a blender with 2 scoops of Oat milk Vanilla Ice Cream. Add a handful of ice and blend until smooth. Serve immediately with sugared dates as a garnish.

Mosaic Coconut Milk (Non-Dairy)

How to make it:

- Prepare three flavors of jello packets by instructions. Such as Pineapple, Cherry, and Blue Wave
- 1-2 Quarts of Vanilla Oat milk
- 1 can of unsweetened coconut milk + 2-3 parts water to coconut milk
- 1 Teaspoon of ground cinnamon
- A dash of Maraschino cherry juice for color and a hint of pink
- 2 tablespoons of monk fruit stevia (or more if you like it sweeter

In a pitcher, mix together oat milk, coconut milk, water, cinnamon, cherry juice, and sweetener. Chill the mixture while the jello sets. When the jello is firm, just slice into cubes and stir into the coconut milk mixture. Pour over ice and enjoy

Red Clover Iced Tea Lemonade

Red clover is believed to have many health benefits and has been studied for years as an herbal supplement. It is a sweet, floral tea that I drink once a day. I found that having it iced and mixed with sugar-free lemonade gives it a delicate floral and citrus flavor. It's so easy and refreshing and helps me get through long, hot summer days.

Ingredients:

- 4 cups of hot water
- 4 tea bags of red clover tea
- 1 liter of sugar-free lemonade
- Ice cubes
- Orange slices for garnish

Pour 4 cups of hot water over 4 bags of red clover tea in a large bowl and allow it to steep for about 30 minutes. In a serving pitcher, put in handfuls of ice cubes and pour the lemonade on top. Once the tea has cooled off, pour it into the pitcher with the lemonade and stir. Chill the tea for about an hour. Pour into a glass with ice and serve.

Cashew Cream Cinnamon "Nog"

I love this non-dairy, egg-free, and potentially sugar-free (if you sub the sugar for monk fruit) "nog". It has got all the festive flavors and creaminess of the traditional punch but friendlier to those with dietary needs. Homemade cashew cream is mixed into "extra creamy" oat milk, which is made by the brand Planet Oat and can be found in the dairy section of your grocery store.

Yields 4-6 8 oz. Glasses.

- 2 ½ cups of whole cashews
- ½ teaspoon of cinnamon
- 1 teaspoon of pure vanilla extract
- 1/8 teaspoon of ground cloves
- 2 tablespoons of sugar
- A pinch of salt
- 1 cinnamon stick
- ½ gallon of Extra Creamy Oat Milk
- Non-dairy whipped topping

Make the cashew cream:
Fill a medium-sized saucepan about halfway full of water. Pour in cashews and bring it to a rolling boil. Allow the cashews to boil for about 10 minutes until they are soft and the liquid is reduced by half. Alternatively, you can soak the cashews in water in the refrigerator overnight to soften them.

Pour off a small amount of the liquid, reserving about half. Put the cashews with the liquid in a blender with the cinnamon, vanilla, ground cloves, sugar, and a pinch of salt. Blend until smooth and creamy. If the texture of the cream is very thick, add a few tablespoons of water and blend until completely smooth. Spoon it into a container to chill for at least 1-2 hours.

In a saucepan, warm the oat milk over medium-low heat. Drop the cinnamon stick in the center and allow it to simmer for 15 minutes. Transfer the oat milk to a pitcher and allow it to chill for 1-2 hours.

Fill a glass about halfway with ice and pour in the oat milk. Add 1-2 spoonfuls of the cashew cream and stir to combine. Top with non-dairy whipped topping and sprinkle cinnamon on top to garnish.

When I think of Frozen Hot Chocolate, I always think of the famous whimsical restaurant Serendipity 3 from New York City. They opened a small location at Caesar's Palace, which was open for several years. We used to go there and order the frozen hot chocolate, which was like a big cup of hot chocolate in daiquiri form. It was served in a huge sundae glass with a tower of whip cream and chocolate shavings with two straws and a spoon. Though Serendipity isn't in Vegas anymore, we can make an easy and fun version at home. I am a great lover of Mexican hot chocolate, so I decided to put a spin on it with a little spice.

Serves 4
- 4 oz. of bittersweet chocolate, cut into chunks
- ½ tablespoon of cocoa powder
- 2 tablespoons of sugar
- ½ cup of half and half
- 3 cups of whole milk
- ¼ cup of Cajeta
- 1 teaspoon of vanilla extract
- 4 cups of ice

In a microwave-safe bowl, melt the bittersweet chocolate in the microwave for 1 minute. If the chocolate is not completely melted, microwave it for another 15 seconds and stir while it finishes melting. Whisk in the cocoa powder, sugar, half and half, vanilla, and cajeta.

In a blender cup, add 2 cups of the ice and 1 ½ cups of the milk. Spoon in about half of the chocolate mixture and blend until it is thick and smooth. Pour into two glasses. Repeat the process for the second two glasses. Serve with whipped topping and a cinnamon stick.

Cold Brew with Salted Honey Whip

A twist on your morning coffee routine

1 Cup of instant cold brew prepared

Salted Honey Whip

- 1 cup of heavy cream
- ¼ confectioners' sugar
- ¼ tsp of fine sea salt
- 3 second pour of desert honey

Combine all ingredients in a large mixing bowl. With a stand mixer with a whisk attachment or a hand mixer. Beat heavy cream mixture until stiff peaks. Dollop on top of milkshakes, coffees or desserts.

ACKNOWLEDGMENTS

I would like to dedicate this book to my sweet Elliot. Nothing in life I will ever do will compare to being your mommy.

My deepest thanks to Taylor, my family - my mother Sharon my father Lawrence, my sister Amy, and my Aunt Janie. Desiree and Allex, without whom I would never have done anything cool or wouldn't ever have any stories to tell.

To my fellow nurses and first responders, especially here in Las Vegas - you survive the unimaginable and make it look easy. I know it's not.

Special thanks to Mary K. Desellems, and Rachel Lunt, Amy Ramsey for recipe testing and
Recipe revising. My thanks go out to Chelsea Cole (A Duck's Oven), Carly Jayne and The Cookbook Lab family for the tools and inspiration to help me bring this book to life. All my love and gratitude to those that have followed along and supported me on social media. Without you all, this book would just be a dream!

And lastly, I love many many cooks and chefs but I give my thanks to Anthony Bourdain, as my creative inspiration. I wish he was here to reign in the "insufferable food nerds" as he once did. May he rest peacefully.

ABOUT THE AUTHOR

Elizabeth Wescott is the Author and Publisher of Desert Honey: Recipes of Comfort and Nostalgia by a Desert Rat, as well as the upcoming title Neon City Treats. She is the creator and owner of Desert Honey Project LLC (www.deserthoney-project.com) and lives in Henderson, Nevada. She was born in Rochester Hills Michigan in 1988 and moved to Las Vegas when she was 10 years old. She spent her childhood and high school years studying music and acting. She is a mother of one worked as a professional baker for four years while attending University of Nevada-Las Vegas. She earned a Bachelor of Science in Kinesiology and a Bachelor of Science in Nursing from Roseman University of Health Sciences and has worked as a trauma nurse in Las Vegas for 5 years. She spends her free time talking about cooking, playing with the kids, browsing restaurant supply stores, watching people make tortillas, food blogging, recipe developing, and playing on her phone. She speaks mostly in movie quotes but is working to limit this. She is a supporter of No Kid Hungry and Every Baby Counts NV and advocates for children and vulnerable adults in her community.

INDEX

A

Abarriata Chili
52
Acai bowls
138
Active dry yeast
86,87,91,94,100,102,124,135,140
Air pockets
27
Airtight container
11,83,97,117,130
Aluminum foil
27
Amino acids
22
Amy's Lazy Braciole
35
Amy's Meyer Lemon cookies
109,110
Appetizer
9,11,14,27
Apple cider vinegar
16,107
Apple swan
138
Argentinian wine
20
Aroma
106
Arroz con leche
23,106
Artichoke leaves
4
Asian markets
57
Avocado
11

B

Baby crackers
6
Back-pocket recipes
45
Bacon
40,45,69
Bagel seasonings
100
Baked bosc pear
108
Baked pears
107
Baking powder
52,97,110,131
Baking sheet
27,50,94,100,110,125,140
Baking soda
94,111,131
Baking spray
50,52,91,122
Balsamic vinegar
43

Bamboo steamer
25,60,71,95
Barbecue rub
81
Bean and bacon soup
40
Beef short ribs
43
Bees
22
Beijing noodle house
48
Beijing noodle style
48
Beluga caviar
6
Bench scraper
125
Berries
111
Bittersweet chocolate
150
Black beans
59
Black caviar
6
Black lumpfish
6
Black sesame oil
25,72
Blistered shishito peppers
22
Blog
23,115
Blue corn fried okra
7
Blue cornmeal
7,138
Blue spirulina
138
Blueberry cream cheese babka
87
Boiled icing
119
Boiled russet potatoes
37
Bosc pears
107
Bouillon granules
63
Bowfin caviar
6
Box mix cake
134
Braised short rib
43
Bratwurst in puff pastry
9
Breadcrumbs
35,48,50,63,68
Bread flour
86,91,94,100,131,135
Broccoli spears
63
Brownies
119
Bun
84,94
Bundt pan

111
Butter
37,52,53,56,61,63,65,66,
68,69,80,81,83,84,86,87,
89,90,91,110,111,114,117,
119,124,125,127,131,134,
135,140
Buttercream
20

C

Cacao nibs
138
Cajeta
150
California roll
11
Campbell's chicken broth
66
Canned beans
40
Canned escargots
56
Canola
43
Caramel
106,115
Cashew cream cinnamon
148
Casserole dish
66,68
Cast iron skillet
4,7,9,14,22,41,48,52,97

Cavatappi shells
84
Cayenne
52,69,150
Celery stalks
40
Ceramic grill
79
Champagne vinegar
72
Charcoal briquettes
79
Charcoal smoker
81
Charitable spirit
21
Cheddar cheese
20,93,68,69,84
Cheese-pull
37
Chef
20,21,23
Chicken bouillon granules
63
Chicken breasts
63
Chicken broth
40,43,66
Chicken divan
63
Chicken katsu
48
Chicken soup
68
Chicken thighs

48
Chinese hot mustard vinaigrette
71
Chinese restaurants
48
Chocolate chip cookies
131
Chocolate chunks
131
Chocolate glaze
119
Chocolate shavings
150
Chopped cilantro
52
Chopped onions
65
Chopped parsley
56,69
Chopped pecans
115,117
Chorizo dogs with black bean whip
59
Chorizo sausages
59
Chuck roast
35
Ciabatta rolls
84
Cilantro pesto
73,74
Cinnamon sticks
106
Cloves
25,35,40,43,45,53,56,65,69,148
Coachella valley date shake
144
Coarse salt
7,35,61,71
Cocktail sauce
81
Cocoa beans
106
Cocoa powder
150
Coconut extract
124,134
Coffee
106,151
Coldbrew
151
Confectioners' sugar
107,151
books
20,23
Cookie dough
110,127
Cooking methods
21
Cooking spray
50,86
Corn meal
52
Corn starch
122
Corn tortillas
17
Cornmeal
7,53,138

Cotija cheese
59,74,
Crab boil
81
Crab cakes
69
Crab mix
11
Crab restaurant
81
Cracked pepper
35
Crap mixture
11
Cream cheese
27,87,89,90
Crushed red pepper
14,52
Cumin
59
Custard base
115

D

Dark brown sugar
80,115,131
David Chang
71
Depression era
21
Desert flowers
22
Desserts
106,107,151
Diced tomatoes
35
Dijon mustard
9
Dinner table
21
Dipping sauces
9
Dough balls
94,95,100,102,125,135
Dough hook attachment
86,100,140
Dragon fruit
114
Dried oregano
14,35
Drizzle soy sauce
11
Dry yeast
86,87,91,94,100,102,124,
135,140
Duke's mayonnaise
20
Duncan hines white cake
134
Dutch oven
40,43,53,71,125,140

E

Easy pasta Carbonara
45
Edamame spaghetti with cilantro pesto
73

Egg whites
50,134
Egg-free
148
Eggplant parmesan
50
Elbow macaroni
84
Elote cornbread
52
Escargots shells
56
Espresso
144
European-style butter
56
Evaporated milk
115,117,119

F

Family recipes
21
Fermentation
102
Festive flavors
148
Feta cheese
27
Filipino hot dogs
57

Fine sea salt
97,102,107,151
Finely minced
11,14,25
Fire grilled artichokes with aioli
4
Flaky sea salt
22
Flat-leaf parsley
43
Floral tea
146
Flour tortillas
97
Fluffy yeast donut
140
Foil molds
134
Food bloggers
23
Food grocery
56
Food intolerances
122
Fork-tender
4,35,37
French shallot mousse
6
Fresh garlic
65
Fresh parsley
14,43,81
Fresh thyme
14,61
Freshly grated parmesan cheese
35,50
Freshly squeezed lemon juice

122
Fried chicken sandwiches
20
Fried eggs
57
Fried panela with herbs
14
Fried spam
24
Frozen broccoli spears
63
Frozen hot chocolate
150
Fry okra
7,138
Frying donuts
100
Full-fat coconut milk
122
Furikake seasoning
57

G

Ganny's pound cake
111
Garlic cloves
35,56
Gerber baby crackers
6
Ghirardelli chocolate chips
131
Giant California roll
11
Giblets
61
Gigantic sundae
41
Glorious mac
84
Gluten-free graham crackers
122
Golden monk fruit
144
Granulated sugar
100,110,111,140
Grated parmesan cheese
35,45,50,65
Gravy
35,43,61
Green egg
79
Green peppers
22
Green tea ice cream
114
Grilled cheese
20
Grilled fish
16
Grilled pimento cheese sandwich 41
Ground beef
53
Ground cinnamon
115,145
Ground cloves
148
Ground pork
25
Gummy texture
86

H

Hamburger style
95
Hard-boiled egg yolks
127
Heat-proof bowl
144
Heavy whipping cream
6,37,115
Heavy-bottomed pot
125
Heirloom tomato salad
16
Herbal supplement
146
Hershey's syrup
119
High-volume baking
20
Hoisin sauce
25
Holy Gospel BBQ rub
80
Homemade
59,102,148
Honey mustard
9
Honey smoked spareribs
79
Honey toast
114
Hoover dam
22
Horseradish
43
Hot grill
4
Hot mustard vinaigrette
71,72
Hot pozole
21

I

Ice cream parlor
40
Icing sheets
135

Italian breadcrumbs
35,50

J

Janie's rice
66
Japanese cuisine
114
Japanese milk bread
91
Japanese restaurant
114
Jaques Pépin
138
Jar of caviar
6

Jarred horse-radish
43

K

Kamado
79
Katsu sauce
48
Kinder's seasoning
80

L

Laura's crispy
17
Leche quemada ice cream
115
Lemon juice
4,9,69,81,87,90,110,122,
Lemon turmeric tart
122
Lemon wedges
81
Lemon zest
110
Lemonade
146
Lighter eggplant parmesan
50
Lime juice
14,52,74,130,134
Linguine noodles
65
Loaf pans
86,89,91
Long-grain white rice
66,106
Low-sodium chicken broth
43
Lump coals
79
Luxurious pasta
45
M
Mac n' Cheese
84
Manteca pork lard
97
Maple syrup
107,122
Maraschino cherry juice
145
Margarine
111,127
Marinara
35,50,52
Marinara sauce
35,50
Marshmallow cream
115,117
Marshmallow fluff
134

Masago
11
Maseca Azul
7
Mashed potatoes
36,37,66
Meat church bbq
80
Meat thermometer
48,140
Medicine
22
Melted butter
93,81,83,91,125,140
Mesh strainer
60
Metaphor
94
Mexican burnt milk candy
115
Mexican crema
52
Mexican food
21
Mexican frozen hot chocolate
149
Mexican hot chocolate
150
Meyer lemon
90,109,110
Meyer lemon babka
90
Michelin-starred restaurants
21
Microwave-safe bowl
150
Mint leaves
130
Miss Moffet's brownies
119
Mochi donuts
123
Mojito mint leaves
130
Molcajete
130
Mom's clam linguini
65
Monk fruit stevia
145
Mosaic coconut milk
145
Mozzarella cheese
35,37

N
Neapolitan crust
102
Neutral oil
43
Non-stick spray
91
O

Oat flour

122
Oat milk vanilla ice cream
144
Old bay seasoning
65
Olive oil herb
14
Onion jam
83
Orange blossom cream honey
90

P
Panela basket cheese
14
Panko breadcrumbs
48,50,68
Paprika
52,84
Paring knife
4,135
Parmesan cheese
35,37,45,50,65,66
Parmesan mashed potatoes
45,37

Pasta Carbonara
45
Pasta noodles
35
Pecorino Romano cheese
45
Perfect sushi rice
23,35
Pillowy softness
91
Pimento cheese
20,41
Pimento grilled cheese
15
Pineapple
138,145
Pineapple slices
138
Pink Himalayan salt
14,16
Pinto beans
40,53,59
Pizza cutter
9
Pizza dough
99,101,102
Ponzu
25
Poppy seeds
9,100
Pork fat
59,94,97

Port of subs
131
Potato masher
37
Pullman pan
91

Punta Cana
23
Pure maple syrup
107
Pursuit
102
Puréed
6

Q

Queso fresco
52

R

Rainbow carrot
2
Ramen
107
Rao's marinara sauce
35
Raw unfiltered desert honey
138
Receptacle
97
Red bell peppers
53
Red clover
146
Red clover iced tea lemonade
146
Red wine
43
Restauranteurs
22
Rib bones
80
Rice wine vinegar
60
Risotto
66

Roast chicken
61
chicken divan
63
Roasted carrots
27
Roasted garlic
27
Rolling boil
100,117,119,148
Round tart pan
122
Rugged bakery
20

S

Safflower oil
124
Saigon cinnamon
144

Salmon roe
6
Salted honey whip
107,108,151

Salty feta whip
27
Sausage
9,57,59
Sautee onions
65
Savory slow braise
35
Scallions
25
Seasonings
14,81,100
Seaweed
11,24
Semi-sweet chocolate chips
119
Serving platter
114,122
Sesame seeds
11,25,111
Shaggy
71
Shallot mouse
6
Sharp cheddar cheese
20,68,70,184
Shredded coconut
106
Shredded Mexican cheese blend
17
Shredded mozzarella cheese
37
Shredded sharp cheddar cheese
84
Shuseki
114
Simple heirloom tomato salad
16
Sizzling fried cheese
14
Smoked crab legs
81
Smokey ketchup sauce
9
Soup simmer
40
Sour cream
52,68,111
Spaghetti noodles
45
Spam musubi
24
Spanish rice
106
Spicy chili crunch
57
Spicy tomato-based pasta sauce
52
Spirulina powder
138

Square dumpling wrappers
25
Squash casserole
68
St. Louis pork spareribs
80
Strawberries
114
Sushi rice
11,24,48,57,60
Sweet chili pepper
22
Sweet onion
52

T

Tailgating-style
9
Tangzhong
91
Taqueria
22
Tastebuds
114
Temperature probe
61,80
Teriyaki sauce
24
Thawed puff pastry
27
The sub shop cookie
131
Thick-cut bacon
69
Toasted oat flour
122
Toasted tomato sandwich
16
Tomato gravy
35
Tortillas
17,59,97
Tostada-like snack
17
Traditional braciola
35
Traditional lemon custard
122
Tupperware bowl
11
Turmeric
122

U

Ube ice cream
114
Unsalted butter
37,81,83,87,91,110,119,124,135
Unsweetened coconut milk
145

V

Vanilla bean ice cream
114
Vanilla bean pan dulce
135
Vanilla extract
106,111,115,119,122,124,130,131,148,150,
Vanilla pudding
131
Vegetable oil
7,17,48,71,100,125,134,140

Virgin olive oil
4,14,22,65,102

W

Walnuts
74,117
Whipped cream cheese
27
Whipped feta tart
27
Whipping cream
6,37,115
White wine vinegar
83
Whole cashews
148
Wonton wrappers
25
Worcestershire sauce
9,53
World war ii
24

Y

Yeast
86,87,91,94,100,102,124,125,135,139,140
Yellow corn
7,138
Yellow mustard
80
Yellow onions
83
Yukon gold potatoes
61

Z

Zest
90,110,122,130

www.ingramcontent.com/pod-product-compliance
Lightning Source LLC
Chambersburg PA
CBHW061407010526
44119CB00011B/280